BEFORE AND AFTER
INTERIORS

BEFORE AND AFTER
INTERIORS

EBURY PRESS·LONDON

Before and After Interiors was conceived, edited and designed by Grub Street, 4 Kingly Street, London W1R 5LF

Published by Ebury Press National Magazine House 72 Broadwick Street London W1V 2BP

First impression 1985

ISBN 0 85223 441 4

Printed and bound in Italy by G. Canale & C. S.p.A. via Tripoli 97 - Turin Phototypesetting by Georgia Ltd, Liverpool

Contents

Very many thanks to all those people who kindly let us view their homes—we're sorry we did not have space to feature more of them. Also special thanks to Robin Bicknell, Carolyn Chapman and Victor Watts for all their help.

Introduction

*T*his book shows how ugly ducklings become swans: how rooms which were initially unpromising were transformed into good-looking and comfortable places to live in. The 'before' pictures are intended not only to show how bad things were to begin with, but also to give hope to those who may be faced with 'doing up' a room at home—it may not be the impossible case it seems. Some of the rooms photographed were near-derelict before their transformation; others had been decorated, but certainly not to their best advantage.

The conversions featured are on two levels, to suit different needs. There are those for home owners with limited resources who are looking for purely decorative changes, and those for people with more time and money who would like to make the drastic changes which come with replanning and structural alterations.

Before and After Interiors is divided into sections dealing with each main room of a home—bedroom, kitchen, bathroom and so on—with an extra section on open living, an increasingly popular form of home design, where most of the day-to-day activities take place in one large area. Each room is shown in its initial state by means of 'before' pictures or plans; where possible, these also show from which angle the

BEFORE

main 'after' photograph was taken, so that exact comparisons can be made. The text then follows through the steps involved in making the various transformations.

In between the main sections are double-page features on the decorative possibilities of such specific and relevant subjects as floors, tiles and windows. And finally, there are pages of step-by-step instructions showing how to follow some of the particularly striking features demonstrated in the book as well as additional impressive and inexpensive techniques such as sandblasting and use of hammered paints. sandblasting and use of hammered paints.

A deliberate cross section of styles is presented throughout, ranging from the most modern of interiors to the more traditional—in fact, something to suit all tastes.

The owners of each scheme are themselves just as varied. Many are professionally involved in design and architecture and therefore bring a keen visual sense and expert ideas to their home decorating.

Before and After Interiors offers a host of imaginative and practical ideas to emulate. Now it's up to you.

Floor plans are used throughout the book to show how the more complicated conversions were carried out.

AFTER

KITCHENS

INDUSTRIAL SIMPLICITY

BEFORE CLUTTERED MISH—MASH

AFTER CLEAN-LINED MODERN KITCHEN

A jumble (above) but a kitchen nonetheless and one more than ready for a clean design sweep.

The new occupants of this period house wanted a smart, modern kitchen along sharp, crisp lines but were keen to achieve it without disturbing the architectural details of the old building. The only really major structural work involved blocking off one doorway—there had been two—and widening the other one to accommodate a wide sliding screen. This alteration effectively opens up the kitchen space and, because the screens are made from translucent perspex sheets with an interior wooden frame, lets light filter in from the hall even when the screens are closed. Interestingly, the architect owner finds conventional doors 'too abrupt' and thinks that sliding doors allow a gradual introduction to a room—while acting as valuable space-savers.

To avoid too much disturbance of the room's mouldings and other architectural details, the owners installed an American metal storage system designed for the catering trade. Its steel framework forms the central island unit which houses the 'floating' hob (at one point there was going to be an extractor hood, also with a flexible tube, which would have led out through the window) and the shelving is also used as a lighting track onto which spotlights are fixed, thereby leaving the surface of the plasterwork undisturbed.

The lower cupboards are made to design and are of an aluminium-faced board cut to size and edged with black plastic and finished with simple handles.

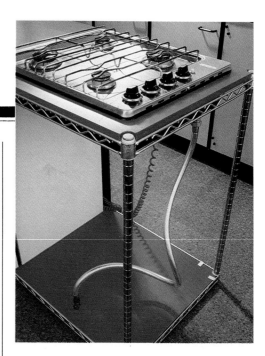

A hob unit installed with pleasing originality (above). The cupboards fitted around the kitchen (right) are shallower than normal to provide more space for the island unit and allow more efficient everyday use. Base units are usually too deep for easy-access storage.

The oven is fitted into a chimney breast and the hard, metal surfaces are offset with cheery, red laminate. At the opposite end of the room a fireplace was removed to gain more space, but the grate was kept in working order. For eating, there is a modern round dining table with red fold-away chairs which can be conveniently hung away when they are not all in use.

In common with many of the other kitchens in the book, this one shows there are all manner of interesting and often cheaper alternatives to off-the-peg kitchens.

CLEAN CUT

BEFORE TWO SEPARATE ROOMS

AFTER A SMALL KITCHEN OPENING OUT ONTO LIVING ROOM

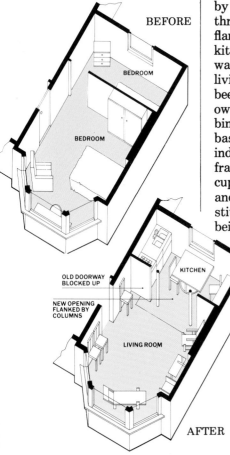

BEFORE

BEDROOM

BEDROOM

OLD DOORWAY
BLOCKED UP

NEW OPENING
FLANKED BY
COLUMNS

KITCHEN

LIVING ROOM

AFTER

Two separate rooms were made into one by blocking off a doorway and knocking through an opening which was then flanked by two narrow columns. The kitchen is arrayed down two opposing walls which makes it less visible from the living room. Much attention to detail has been paid to its construction by the owner and he has used an unusual combination of commercial materials: the base units have doors fronted in industrial grey rubber flooring and framed with aluminium strip; the wall cupboards have plastic roller shutters and the working surface is of reconstituted granite tiles which, instead of being grouted in the usual way, are separated with matchstick-thin strips of aluminium. The splashback is a sheet of stainless steel left

Re-siting and enlarging the opening between two rooms (left) created a sunnier living space as light now streams in from both ends of the large room. Interesting surfaces abound in the kitchen (above): rubber, granite, plastic, stainless steel, aluminium and hammered, stove enamelled paint.

undisturbed by the usual row of kitchen sockets for appliances. The owner finds the look of these unaesthetic and as a result has secreted them on the under side of the wall units on the sink side (well away from water); on the opposite side they are surface-mounted on the working surfaces and hidden with protective metal plates.

The stove is an old one which was dismantled and transformed by being stove enamelled an iron grey. The stainless steel floor, which has a slight crazed pattern on it, is a left-over from an exhibition and has been carefully extended beyond the kitchen into the living area so that the two rooms are more visually linked. Note that all the skirting boards have been removed (as have the window architraves, see page 48) to emphasize the room's clean cut and uncluttered lines. At the window are Roman blinds which employ a neat idea worth copying: their operating cord is held by a yacht-racing cleat which replaces the laborious job of winding the cord round a hook. Finally, the dining table (the owner's design) is topped for the moment by a type of reconstituted board but will one day have a thick, etched glass top.

OLD WITH NEW

BEFORE DINING ROOM WITH WINDOW LOOKING ONTO A LEAN-TO KITCHEN

AFTER KITCHEN WITH FRENCH WINDOWS LEADING TO A PATIO

A town kitchen (above left and above) but one which has a little of the air of an old-fashioned dairy. Original fittings such as the hearth combine with modern versions of traditional flooring, cupboards, pail (used as a rubbish bin) and so on.

The rickety wooden back extension which used to house the kitchen (really nothing more than a stone sink and a pre-war electric cooker) was knocked down and turned into a small patio destined one day to be the foundations of a conservatory/dining room. The sash window (removed before the photograph on the left was taken) was replaced with a pair of secondhand French windows that were not only cheaper than new ones but had the kind of attractive fittings which are no longer easy to come by. Architectural salvage places are good hunting grounds for anyone doing up an old house and can usually provide something more interesting than the local DIY super-store.

The kitchen range already existed elsewhere in the house, covered with years of paint; it was moved, sand-blasted, then polished up with stove black. This and the old doors provided the starting point for a traditional style of kitchen, one that calls for an old-fashioned cooker rather than a split oven and hob. The owner dislikes fitted kitchen units, particularly wall ones, so these were kept to an absolute minimum with an 8 ft (2·5 m) span of bottom cupboards only, inexpensively constructed from a kind of medium-density chipboard to form panels, painted and then topped with tiles. Above them is a very thick, open shelf—originally a builder's plank—and pictures to look at when doing the washing up: much more interesting than rows of blank-faced cupboards.

Letting in light

There are no cornices or interesting architectural details and the room is slightly below ground level, so the light source is not as bright as it could be. To counteract these conditions, the ceiling was painted bright white, as was the top 2 ft (0·6 m) or so of wall. This was stopped at a decorative border which adds interest to the otherwise plain walls. A strip of the same border also emphasizes the beading which runs round the working surface. Reflecting against the ceiling is another light surface, the traditional white with

black marble-look floor (here it is synthetic but it could always be painted, using gloss or tile paint if you have the time and patience). To bounce even more valuable light into the room, a mirror has been placed on the kitchen table wall opposite the French windows so that garden greenery is reflected to diners. Mirrors really can work transformation miracles of light and space in small rooms.

Substituting glass for solid surfaces

can also make a surprising difference: the old cupboard in the corner was fairly unattractive, but rather than rip it out the owner substituted the top panels with glass so that it immediately looked more like a decorative dresser. It was then given a special paint technique finish (called dragging) and new handles. The same method can be applied in dark halls or rooms where door panels can be replaced with glass to let in light and open up a new perspective.

A town kitchen (left) but one which has a little of the air of an old-fashioned dairy. Original fittings such as the hearth combine with modern versions of traditional flooring, cupboards, pail (used as a rubbish bin) and so on.

13

FAMILY EFFICIENCY

BEFORE THREE SMALL GROUND-FLOOR ROOMS

AFTER A MONOCHROMATIC, GALLEY KITCHEN

BEFORE

DOOR TO OUTSIDE

KITCHEN/DINER

KITCHEN

LARDER

PAVED BACK GARDEN

NEW GLASS DOOR INTO LIVING ROOM

KITCHEN

PLAY AREA FOR CHILDREN

WINDOW

PART OF OLD WALLS RETAINED TO SCREEN FREEZER, ETC

FREEZER AND STORAGE AREA

CONSERVATORY

AFTER

A convivial place for the family to congregate was what was required from an unpromising long, narrow space, about 3 metres (9 ft) created by knocking together three small rooms. It has worked very successfully (the dartboard and fruit machine are no doubt an extra draw) and even when there is no-one around the person cooking can see what's going on in the living room via a new glass-panelled door. A new window above the sink also provides a handy viewpoint into the combined conservatory/play-room to check on what the children are up to.

The only really expensive items included in the whole conversion are the

Three rooms into one did go, but still left a long, narrow space (left). Despite its shape, the kitchen works efficiently—and socially. Sturdy metal bars (right) form a skeleton for hanging kitchen storage.

floor tiles. The low cupboards are simply engineering brick uprights with doors put onto them and painted black inside. To break up the rectangular look of the kitchen the doors are laminated with black curves and the result is far more characterful than anything that could have been bought ready-made for the room. Uncompromising heavy metal bars provide plentiful storage for equipment, mugs, etc., which are hung on butchers' hooks. For a softer look along the same slatted lines, you could use lengths of wood.

Following through the white, black, grey theme, the working top is stainless steel to match two round sinks, beside which is a chopping board, also round to help counteract all the straight lines. The chopping board has a very handy central hole and bung, which can be removed to allow vegetable peelings to be scraped through into the rubbish bin below. Two children can just squeeze on stools to eat at this end of the worktop. Utility equipment and fridges are at the far end of the kitchen, effectively screened by the walls which were partially retained during conversion.

CHEERFUL 'N' CHEAP

BEFORE LOFT SPACE

AFTER MULTI-COLOURED BUDGET KITCHEN

The corner of a large and empty loft space (above) provided the bare bones from which the architect defined the new kitchen (right).

Cheapness was the overriding factor for this kitchen. It had to be built on a very low budget, which the architect achieved by this simple design. First, a stud partition wall was erected to cut diagonally across the corner of the room. This breaks up the rigidity of the corner and provides a convenient place to hide the washing machine and dryer. It will also provide the entrance to a balcony one day.

The storage units were simply constructed from blockboard and then painted by the owner, who made a virtue out of her admitted lack of decorating skill. She wanted to use three pastel colours but knew fiddly painting was not her forté and so simply ran one colour indiscriminately into another for an unusual and pretty effect (see left and right). The working surface comprises a checkerboard of terracotta and black quarry tiles which are edged with multi-pastel quarter-round tiles in the same hues as the cupboards. The depth of the working surface was determined by a stainless steel top found in a junk shop.

Functional fixtures

The owner much prefers ordinary fittings, hating any that have been redesigned out of existence into ugly, unnecessary contortions. Consequently, taps, handles and lighting are straightforward and functional. She chose the same approach for the open storage above the units; shelves are supported by uncompromising hardware store brackets, the shelves themselves painted shiny red on their upper surfaces and matt grey underneath. Left as natural wood, which most of us would have been tempted to do, they would have lost their impact entirely. The triangular corner around which they are arrayed helps to define the kitchen's cooking area.

Other unusual details which complete the idiosyncratic style of this kitchen are the old-fashioned radiators rescued from a factory and the undecorated beams. The quirkiest touch of all—planned for the future—is to wrap a rope around the cast iron pillar and add foliage at the top. The kitchen will then have its very own palm tree to breakfast under.

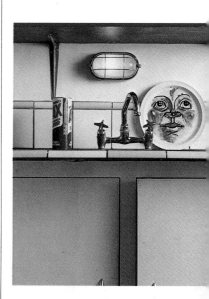

Multi-coloured pastel tiles and paint (above) enliven and soften the simply—and cheaply—constructed cupboards and shelves of the loft kitchen (left) which otherwise might have been too aggressively workman-like.

FIFTIES NOSTALGIA

BEFORE
VICTORIAN MANSION
APARTMENT ROOM

AFTER
NOSTALGIC
FIFTIES-STYLE
KITCHEN

A handsome window—but one with no view—was the only interesting architectural detail in an otherwise featureless room (above). Out of this a nostalgic style kitchen was created (right).

Inspired by the kind of kitchen Doris Day was constantly to be found busying herself in during the Fifties and early Sixties, this room was an antidote to the kitchen in the owner's old home, which was ultra-modern and very hard-edged with terrazzo, metal and matt ceramic tiles—showy to look at but not particularly easy to work in. This time he wanted a comfortable kitchen with lots of cupboard space and a central table; straightforward and practical but with an original twist. An old Doris Day film on television provided the theme he needed and a picture of her in a magazine supplied the colour scheme.

Powder blue and primrose yellow were the evocative main colours, perked up with an orangey tan on the larder and main door. When planning a similar period piece in any room it's best to check out first what were the popular colours of the time. These will capture the right atmosphere at once. In this kitchen the units are up to date but anonymous enough not to have a specific look, so with the addition of an archetypal Fifties blue laminate top they immediately change character. Luckily the laminate manufacturers still make a few old shades, as do the manufacturers of the standard (and inexpensive) plain wall tiles.

Cooking in style

Finding a suitable period cooker presented a problem (separate hob and oven units were obviously out) as modern-day designs are much more streamlined, with all sorts of space-age digital displays and smoked brown trims which would definitely not be in keeping. At first the solution was to buy a second-hand cooker, but this did not work efficiently enough so the owner bought the least offensive cooker he could find, stripped its modern trims and painted those parts pale blue with a car spray.

On the floor are the typical vinyl tiles so popular in the Fifties; the chairs match in style, and the table—a classic from earlier times—fits in well. All that is needed to complete the Doris Day look is a pair of frilled gingham curtains; or, alternatively, Rock Hudson.

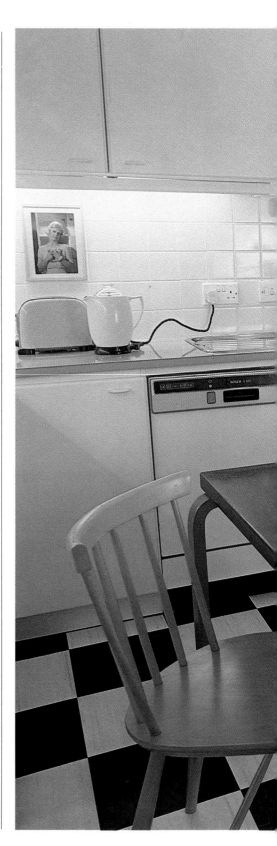

Framed in all her glory above a period-piece toaster, Doris Day smiles out from her own film studio kitchen into the Fifties style one she inspired (left). The small appliances are all true to the era, picked up from junk shops and old electrical corner shops.

BARE BRICK

BEFORE AN UNTOUCHED TURN-OF-THE-CENTURY KITCHEN

AFTER A MODERNIZED KITCHEN WITH DINING EXTENSION

Untouched since the Thirties, the old kitchen (above) was a muddle of pipes and chipped white tiles.

The kitchen in this house was too small for family eating and cooking, so it was decided to take out the end wall and replace it with a lofty dining area. The new construction was planned to include a garage and lavatory, the whole building extending as far as the garden fence. Windows and doors afford a good view of the garden and the owners took full advantage of this, making a pond which butts right up to the window. Now the daily comings and goings of the newts and goldfish can be observed in leisurely fashion from the dining table.

Bare brick has been utilized a lot in the new design because it links with the exterior of the old house and because it creates attractive arches, which the owners feel have been out of fashion for a long time and are due for a comeback. The brickwork is interspersed with new cupboard doors made of tongue and groove and backed with ply, and with old cupboards like the one above the sink which was a junk shop find. There is deliberately plenty of display space—to show off the couple's collection of Art Nouveau and Aesthetic Movement pieces. The raised plinth at the back of the blue-tiled working surfaces houses the services and the whole worktop has been made deeper than normal to extend easily over the dishwasher.

The ceiling was lowered and boarded to improve the proportions of the old kitchen. It also succeeds in giving extra contrast to the transition of walking from it into the double height of the dining area.

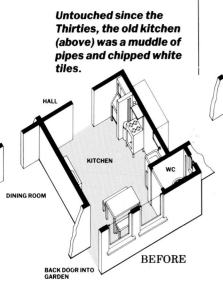

HALL

KITCHEN

WC

DINING ROOM

BEFORE

BACK DOOR INTO GARDEN

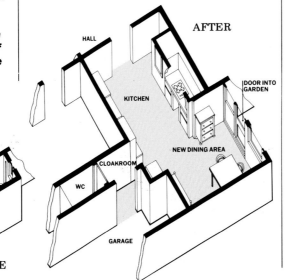

AFTER

HALL

KITCHEN

DOOR INTO GARDEN

CLOAKROOM

WC

NEW DINING AREA

GARAGE

During the redesign the only thing which remained the same was the position of the cooker (far left). The dining extension (left) shows how old and new materials mixed together can create a comfortable and relaxed family kitchen.

COLOUR CODED

BEFORE DINING ROOM EXTENSION

AFTER SUNNY, ALL-PURPOSE FAMILY KITCHEN

The previously dark dining extension, stripped and ready for decorating action (above). The original small window has already been removed and new French doors, in the same style as the other windows of the house, have been substituted. The owners were aware that nothing ruins the atmosphere of an old house more quickly than adding windows out of sympathy with its period and style.

The requirement of this extension was a kitchen with plenty of room for comfortable eating as well as floor space where the children would play without getting in the way—a room to live in, in fact. The result proved to be an area in which the family happily ended up spending most of its time while the rest of the house was being renovated.

Prior to decoration, the window at the far end of the room was removed and French windows into the garden were substituted. The sunny colour scheme came from the directors' chairs, which were primarily chosen for their comfort so that diners could relax over an evening meal or the family watch television, as the case might be.

Sunnyscheme
Everything is in yellow and white, which may be a bit too restrictive for some, but

A simple, easy-to-clean kitchen (left) which relies upon the use of yellow and white to give it impact.

does look effective here: even the white tiles have been yellow grouted. Their square shape is echoed by the wallpaper's grid pattern.

Rather than merely painting the ceiling white, which is what most of us would have been tempted to do, the ceiling here matches the walls. This looks much more effective and holds the decorative scheme together visually.

In the evening, corner uplighters play upon its pattern. A tiled shelf along the dining side of the room matches the working surface's splashback and houses the television and various accessories, leaving the floor space uncluttered by furniture apart from the dining table and chairs.

All these light colours, unfussy lines and easy-clean surfaces have created a light and cheery atmosphere.

COMPACT COOKING

BEFORE
LANDING IN AN
OLD HOUSE

AFTER
COMPACT KITCHEN

The redesign of this home involved changing a bathroom into a kitchen (below) and blocking off a doorway. The opened-out kitchen is now an integral part of the general living area.

Literally a kitchen 'below stairs' and restricted to a $2 \cdot 66\,\text{m} \times 2 \cdot 5\,\text{m}$ ($8 \cdot 5 \times 8 \cdot 2\,\text{ft}$) space, this room has, despite its city location, a relaxed and comfortable air usually associated with more rural surroundings. Virtually an alcove of the adjoining living room, its compactness makes it a practical place to work in as everything is immediately to hand.

Custom-made by a local carpenter in old wood, the new kitchen employs various visual tricks to create a feeling of space: glass-fronted cupboards and open shelves are less oppressive than solid units in a small space and make storage areas appear lighter as well as more visually interesting. Mirror is used as a splashback instead of tiles and is also fitted in a single large piece between two windows and above the peninsular unit. Both mirrors help to open up the area and make it look bigger than it really is.

The kitchen incorporates various clever storage ideas, the most ingenious being a bottomless wall cupboard over the sink. This is fitted with a rack so that washed plates can be put away immediately and allowed to drip themselves dry. A large built-in wine rack at the end of the middle counter (which houses the fridge) is a marvellous store for all sorts of additional necessities of domestic life other than wine: candles, screwdrivers, and other tools are all kept easily to hand. As many of the modern fixtures as possible are hidden behind wooden doors (such as the freezer and the air extractor), while all laundry appliances are sensibly relegated to the bathroom.

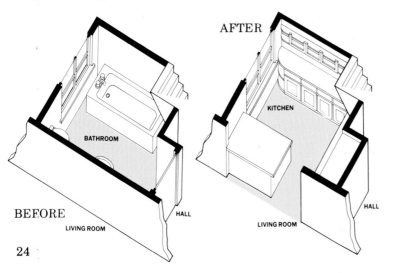

BEFORE

BATHROOM

LIVING ROOM

HALL

AFTER

KITCHEN

LIVING ROOM

HALL

Tucked in under the stairs, this kitchen (left) succeeds in being both extremely compact and relaxed. Clever use of mirror helps to increase the space instantly. The custom-built units are made from old wood.

STYLISH FLOORS

Flooring is one of the home's most important purchases in terms of both expense and looks and it can offer many alternatives to the ubiquitous fitted carpet. It's possible to choose from natural materials such as wood, marble and slate which all improve and mature with age, or be creative with synthetics, metal (see page 34) and so on. Here are some ideas which show what can be done if an individual touch is added to what is readily available on the market.

Wood strip floor laid diagonally (right) to add interest and visually widen a narrow hall.

Vinyl tiles are relatively inexpensive. They are sold in square shapes, but need not be used in this way. It is easy enough to devise an uncomplicated geometric design and, with a sharp knife and ruler, to achieve an effect like this bathroom floor (below).

A stylish painted and faded-look floor makes a welcome change to the stripped and sealed treatment wooden floors are usually given. For method see page 145.

Two rugs to trick the eye. The oriental one (left) would take time and patience, but the result, even down to the realistic ruck, is a painted triumph of trompe l'oeil. Simpler to emulate is the painted border to a real carpet (above) an effect to brighten up any plain rug. (See page 146).

KITCHEN DINERS

BEFORE

AFTER

PLAIN AND SIMPLE

BEFORE
TRADITIONAL TOWN HOUSE BEDROOM

AFTER STYLISH KITCHEN AND DINING ROOM

The old bedroom filled one end of a long, narrow space which the architects opened out and simplified during conversion.

A rather undistinguished and forlorn bedroom (above) was stripped of its architectural detailing and fireplace, something ordinarily frowned upon by many. The resulting kitchen diner (right) could persuade them otherwise.

The new owner of this apartment did not want to keep traditional architectural detailing and so mouldings were either stripped out or covered over. The windows were replaced with modern pivoting ones and the mantelpiece removed so that the fire became a simple opening into the chimney breast with a marble hearth. By removing walls, the room was opened out to the rest of the apartment. One area now flows into another and light floods into the communicating corridor by way of a newly-created skylight.

It was important that the kitchen should not be separated from the dining room by a wall as this would make the two rooms too claustrophobic. Instead they remained combined, with the island sink unit acting as an effective dividing screen between diners and the cooking area. The curving front and counter top softens its presence and ensures that there are no sharp corners against which to bump inadvertently.

Because the kitchen is so blatantly on show, the architects thought its components should resemble furniture more than kitchen units. Hence they are finely but simply made in harmony with the room. There are no unnecessary embellishments; lines are pure with form and texture alone, while warm-coloured tiled and wooden flooring, scattered here and there with simple rugs, helps to give the room its relaxed feel.

SIMPLE COUNTRY

BEFORE THREE SMALL, COTTAGE ROOMS

AFTER OPEN-PLAN COUNTRY LIVING

This simple country kitchen has been converted with the minimum of cost from three rooms, all at slightly different levels. Two were knocked into one and the remaining room—once a lavatory—was turned into a walk-in larder. The back door was changed into a window to let in more light and the flag-stoned floor evened out and polished up with an industrial machine. The basics done, the owner began furnishing with the installation of a solid fuel range. As well as giving warmth and cooking facilities, this also supplies that essential feeling of homeliness necessary for true country kitchens. Unusually positioned between two windows, it combines with the view to make the end wall a natural focal point.

The kitchen units are made of tongue and groove wooden panelling and topped with white tiles, except for one surface which is wooden and inset with marble for pastry making. Simple, inexpensive and effective, they are homemade and demonstrate that style is more to do with ideas than with vast sums of money; with interiors, lack of funds is often the mother of invention and inspiration for original ideas.

A common theme helps to pull together an inexpensively furnished room—in this instance blue and white, which takes its cue from the decorative china displayed on walls and shelves: a

Clutter aplenty, but a unifying blue and white colour scheme (above and right) provides visual excitement to what is basically a plain and simple country kitchen: flagstones, white-washed walls and boarded cupboards.

canny eye for collecting ensures that even a simple row of lids from broken pots can look good. Baskets, bunches of dried flowers and gleaming utensils all add to the busy, homely look that goes to make an ideal country kitchen.

The bare kitchen (above) with solid fuel cooker already installed and cupboards (far right) about to be built. The original two small rooms and hall were opened out into one area and the lavatory transformed into a handy walk-in larder.

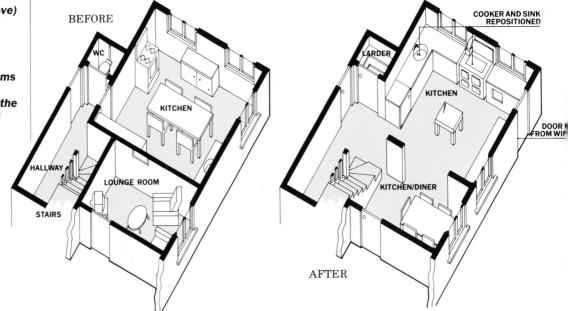

BEFORE

WC

KITCHEN

HALLWAY

LOUNGE ROOM

STAIRS

COOKER AND SINK REPOSITIONED

LARDER

KITCHEN

DOOR FROM WIN

KITCHEN/DINER

AFTER

MODERN COUNTRY

BEFORE COW
BYRE WITH STALLS

AFTER
SOPHISTICATED
COUNTRY KITCHEN

Using the old stone and tiles, the original cow byre was almost entirely rebuilt (above). The new roof beams lacked the character of age and so were painted grey (right) to harmonise with the monochromatic scheme. Greenery— both inside and out—softens the stark lines.

The derelict cow byre that formed the basis of this kitchen was standing, but only just, and had to be knocked down—leaving only a 6 ft (1·8 m) back wall—before being rebuilt. The original openings of the building were kept to the same size and proportion, but replaced with double glazed sliding doors. Although situated in the countryside, the theme of the house is very much *not* the traditional country home: furnishings and fittings are very modern and have a definite Japanese influence to them, with lots of black and natural exotically marked woods, such as olive ash, com-bined with modern Italian design style.

The kitchen, as well as the other quarters (living room and the bedrooms/bathrooms are in an adjoining low, long building), looks out onto a large courtyard via sliding doors. The courtyard is paved with stone flags featuring small terracotta inserts and the kitchen floor has been treated in the same way. Matching the inside to the outside in this manner is a good way of bringing the two areas together visually, and in the summer with the doors open the feeling is of one large indoor/outdoor room. Stone flags are chilly underfoot, however, so the

kitchen also boasts underfloor heating.

The owner was particularly keen that the room should be as unlike a kitchen as possible; he wanted the units to look like pieces of modern furniture and to that end had them custom-made in black-stained ash with olive ash trim. Rather than have the splashback tiled, which would not have suited the textures of the room, he again used olive ash which matches all the flush interior doors. In future, the freestanding unit at the far end of the room will be moved to a new position beside the dining table. This will be done as soon as a doorway is knocked

through to the barn beyond to create another, larger, sitting room.

The colours of the room are fairly neutral—cream and black mixed with natural stone—so to give that necessary extra 'lift' (what the decorators would call an 'accent colour'), the owner has literally added visual sparkle—with liberal use of chrome on the taps, table-ware items and spectacularly on an old French stove which is now used as a bar. A profusion of greenery adds the finishing decorative touch and softens down the room's hard lines, as does the view from the wall of windows.

An old French stove (above), takes on a new lease of life by acting as a bar. Assorted baskets on the wall help to make the area an attractive focal point.

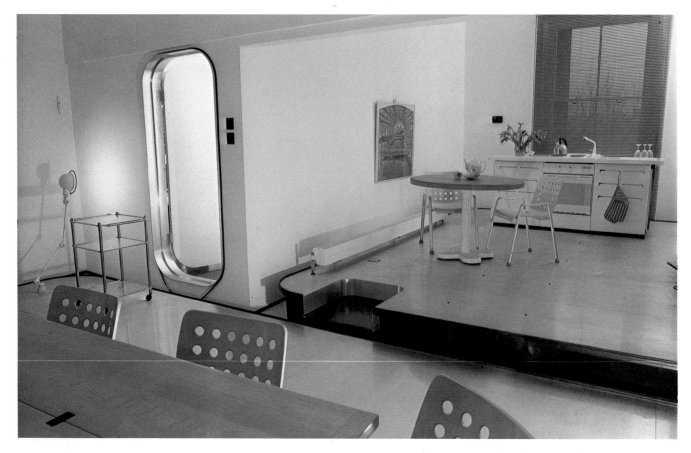

SCULPTURED METAL I

BEFORE TWO
ROOMS AND A
HALLWAY

AFTER COMBINED
KITCHEN/DINING
ROOM

The fundamentals of this apartment's redesign are the raised aluminium platforms and floors which feature in the dining and kitchen areas as well as the bedroom (see page 140). They are part of a deliberately neutral background which the architect intended for the owner so that he could at any time furnish it with any style of furniture or rugs, old or new, and it would take either quite happily. The metal flooring has a raised pattern, but does scratch and weather, as does wood, and is easily kept clean with liquid detergent. The floor is also earthed as it contains the electric sockets.

The wall between the kitchen and the large dining room was knocked down and the kitchen is now only visually separate by being on a higher level. Doorways resemble those watertight bulkheads found on ships.

For once the kitchen sink has not been placed flush to the window, but is situated at right angles to it. The island unit in which it is housed has a seamless top with curved edges which is made from acrylic sheet sprayed with special hardwearing paint.

Within its confines is the dish washer, refrigerator, hob, sink and cooker; slits along its vertical sides provide ventilation as well as hanging space.

Eventually another similarly-shaped unit will be made for the wall to the right of the photograph; the long side will house useful shallow shelves for storage (most base units are too deep for efficient use) and the jutting arm into the room will be a breakfast bar.

The beginnings of building a space-age shell within the framework of an old house (left). The finished result (above and right) is gleamingly simple—metal flooring compared favourably with carpeting in price.

COOL CLASSIC

BEFORE
CHAOTIC,
UNPLANNED
KITCHEN

AFTER
CLASSIC MARBLE
AND WOOD
KITCHEN

Confusion reigned—and strip lighting highlighted it in a most unflattering way in the kitchen above. Its transformation owes as much to new lighting as it does to redesign (above and right). There is no reason why a kitchen should be lit harshly; this mistake, which is very commonly made, can spoil any new decorative scheme.

The old kitchen was in such a jumbled state that it was totally ripped out and the new one carefully planned in order to make it as efficient a machine for cooking in as possible. The thick marble working surfaces have coved backs for easy cleaning and there are two sinks; one for washing up, the other for vegetable preparation. There are also two hob units; one gas and the other (on the peninsular unit) a single electric plate specially installed for breakfast time egg boiling and consequently positioned near to the dining table.

The washing up sequence has also been given two alternatives. A specially made washing up rack means that dishes can either drip-dry or else be put into the dishwasher, but both rack and machine are next to a large custom-built china cupboard so that things can immediately be stacked away. Carefully considered details include a heated rail for drying up cloths (hidden by the cupboard in this picture) and an inset for holding washing up necessities which has been knocked into the disused chimney breast above the sink.

The made-to-measure units are in oak and the floor covered in terracotta flag-stones, both of which will improve as they age. Out of the door on the left are small rooms which house the laundry, larder and an enormous fridge. At the other end of the room an old extension has been knocked down and replaced with a conservatory which is also used as an additional dining room on sunny days.

STYLIZED RURAL

BEFORE TOWN HOUSE ATTIC ROOM WITH SMALL, DORMER WINDOWS

AFTER COUNTRY-STYLE KITCHEN WITH FRENCH WINDOWS

Two dark attic rooms transformed into light-filled ones (below) by the installation of floor-to-ceiling windows and a tiny terrace.

The owner of this house wanted a kitchen/diner which would have a period, cosy kind of country atmosphere despite being in the city. Lots of light and space were essential so initially the small windows were altered by knocking them out and substituting three sets of floor-to-ceiling French windows. Beyond these was added a tiny terrace: only a few feet deep, it is just big enough to stand on but achieves the required effect. The long windows open out the room to the view beyond and when they are thrown open, the room seems at one with the outside.

Another major alteration involved clever juggling of space, from which was gained a largish walk-in larder and general storage area invisible to the eye behind a stud wall. (The same was done to gain a walk-in wardrobe in the adjoining bedroom, see plan.) Tackling a storage space this way is well worth considering: the expense of doors and carpentry for a long run of fitted cupboards is high and the plasterboard partition with one flush door may well work out cheaper. Decorated to match as the rest of the walls it will merge with them—an extra bonus since rows of fitted cupboard doors are not always a partic-

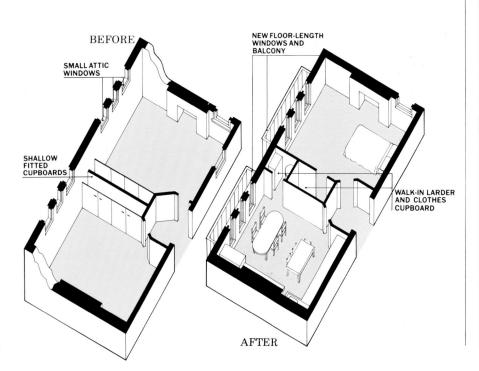

BEFORE

SMALL ATTIC WINDOWS

SHALLOW FITTED CUPBOARDS

NEW FLOOR-LENGTH WINDOWS AND BALCONY

WALK-IN LARDER AND CLOTHES CUPBOARD

AFTER

Made-to-measure kitchen units (above and left) simply but effectively made from wooden frames, perforated metal sheeting and a backing of black-painted block-board which cuts out dust and hides cupboard contents. Tiles, accessories and furniture are true to the rural theme.

ularly attractive sight. The owner, an architect and interior designer, doesn't much care for off-the-peg kitchen units either, finding them too uniform and the proportions all wrong for old houses. She therefore had her kitchen cupboards made to her own design, something else which can work out cheaper if you keep things simple as she did. These grey-painted units are made with cheap wooden frames across which is stretched perforated metal (from a plumber's merchant); behind this is black-painted blockboard which keeps out the dust and shields the view of possibly untidy cupboards. This means they look very much like an old-fashioned meat safe and are topped with a metal working surface like a French bar. It's not cheap but the owner commends it as the best kitchen surface she has ever worked on. There are no drawers as she likes to keep cooking equipment immediately to hand and enjoys seeing utensils displayed. The tiles are grouted grey to match the units and give a professional finish—the grey paint she used was specially mixed for her as she finds that the colours available on the ready-mix paint charts have too harsh a tone to them.

Final polish

An open grate encourages a comfortable, country kitchen atmosphere and the fireplace was built out into the room to make it a more dominant feature. The flooring is brown linoleum, the sort once used to cover school floors. The large dining table is a fake. It is really a small table topped with a large piece of blockboard which was given a lip before the whole piece was stained and polished to build up a deceiving patina. The large cupboard with chicken wire front was originally a pigeon house found by the owner in a market for next to nothing. Once it was cleaned of its bird droppings, she stained both wood and chicken wire a dark brown, then polished it up into an enviable piece of furniture. Simple red check curtains, paintings and a few additional pieces of antique furniture with storm lantern style lighting complete this rural but very stylish theme.

The effect is understated and comfortable, but attention to detail was essential for this room's stylish design: wooden moulding 'finishes off' the join between wall and ceiling; curtains are simple checked fabric but elegantly made and hung; the storage cupboard is an ex-pigeon house which was spotted as having potential.

TILED ZIG-ZAG

BEFORE SMALL BATHROOM, LAVATORY AND KITCHEN

AFTER TILED FAMILY KITCHEN WITH A PARTIALLY SEPARATED DINING ROOM

A warren of small rooms, including a bathroom, was knocked down to create one large kitchen with an efficient but unusually-shaped working surface (far right). Open shelves visually link the stepped-up dining room (above, right) with the cooking area.

A zig-zagged working counter is not a shape that would strike most people as being efficient for a kitchen, but this design has proved otherwise. After knocking down a badly neglected extension of small rooms and then inserting large sliding windows into the replacement building, the architect owner was left with a rectangular room which he could have planned conventionally with two runs of cupboards on opposing walls.

A dislike of standard manufacturers' units, and the fact that there was no space for a large country-style kitchen table in the middle of the room, led him to try another solution: that of custom-made working surfaces with added zig-zag shapes which create built-in triangles of table on each side of the kitchen. With the sink set in at an angle and the marble working surface on the opposite side, the arrangement creates a circular work flow. The sink surface is 90 to 100 mm (3–4 in) higher than the marble top, ensuring comfortable working at both: sinks are often positioned too low resulting in needless back bending for washers-up.

The fronts of the working surfaces were tiled rather than fitted with closed storage, again in an attempt to cut down on the inefficiency of bending over and delving into deep cupboards. Behind the zig-zags are open spaces where the bread-bin, vegetable trugs, rubbish bin and so on are kept on raised steps so that the floor is swept without disturbing them. them.

There are a few fitted wall units, but most of the kitchen table- and cook-ware is decoratively displayed around the room and on long open shelves which extend into the stepped-up dining room to link the two areas visually. The floor at the eating end is wooden to match the dining table. Such natural warm colours complement the browns and natural textures of the cooking area and create a perfect foil for the luxuriant greenery outside, to which the eye is led naturally by a meandering path.

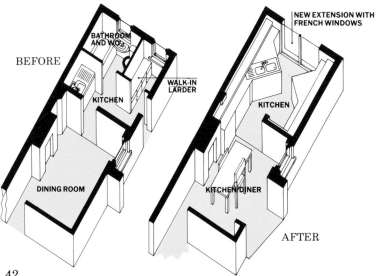

BEFORE

BATHROOM AND WC

WALK-IN LARDER

KITCHEN

DINING ROOM

NEW EXTENSION WITH FRENCH WINDOWS

KITCHEN

KITCHEN/DINER

AFTER

PRACTICAL PARTITION

BEFORE BASIC OPEN LOFT KITCHEN

AFTER SCREENED KITCHEN WITH ADJOINING DINING AREA

Rather than rip out the old kitchen units, the architect of this transformation decided to save money and keep them as the bones of his new design. To make them less obtrusive, however, he gave them a built-in look by installing a fake wall above, and flush with, the wall-hung units.

The kitchen needed to be screened in some way from the rest of the apartment and from the front door, which is adjacent to the fridge. Rather than cut out precious light by building walls, the architect dreamt up a series of pillars with connecting partitions so that although the kitchen is successfully disguised, the sun can still stream in past it. The partitions serve a dual purpose, acting as hidden extra storage on the kitchen side, as do the pillars which house the stereo speakers. A new fake beam on the ceiling between the two uprights is the perfect place for a row of downlighters. If more privacy is required in the kitchen, the open areas between the pillars can be fitted with Venetian blinds or glass shelves, but the beauty of this design is really in its utter simplicity.

The new scheme works perfectly in its intentions; the kitchen has been isolated without cutting it off totally and the dining area is separate but close enough for easy serving across the newly-created, marble-topped working surface. The table already existed in the apartment but it too was given a new lease of life with a white laminate covering to match the all-white theme of the overall design. When the table is butted up to the structure it becomes an integral part of it. The area of white flooring around the cooking appliances which before looked somewhat odd and isolated is now contained and makes sense both practically and visually.

There is no need to rip out a kitchen you don't like; instead, revamp it—as has happened here. New doors were made for the old carcass (above) and the space above the units filled in to give them a more built-in and less obtrusive appearance. Combined with the partition, the new-look kitchen (right) is virtually unrecognizable.

GLAZED OVER

BEFORE OLD
SCULLERY AND
BACK YARD

AFTER STREAM-
LINED KITCHEN
AND GLAZED
DINING ROOM

This redesign filled in part of the L-shape which is common at the back of many a terraced house (above). The extension's glass roof (right and far right) still allows in plenty of light and its erection from ready-made units was relatively straight-forward.

The often rather gloomy L-shape found at the back of many a terraced house has been put to good use by this owner. He glazed over half of the 'L' and made it an integral part of the house, first by blocking off the old door to the scullery and then by replacing a sash window into the living room with a ceiling-high opening. The only access now to the kitchen is through this and via the glass-roofed dining room. The double-glazed roof structure was prefabricated and erected by the owner architect, and the floor was laid in beech strip which links it with that of the living room and the kitchen.

Black to match
The kitchen was completed at very little expense—a fact which belies its stylish black and white appearance. Designed and built by the owner, it has softwood doors fronted with perforated steel which was stove enamelled by an enameller with a textured, hammered-finish paint (see page 148). The worktop has a curved front and back for easy maintenance. The woodwork is stained ebony and to carry through the monochromatic scheme, the white tiled working surface has been grouted in black. There are black mixer taps and, for a fully coordinated picture, even black dining furniture to match.

A simple, monochromatic colour scheme echoes the unfussy lines of the new dining and cooking areas (above and right). Doorless openings allow the separate areas to flow into each other.

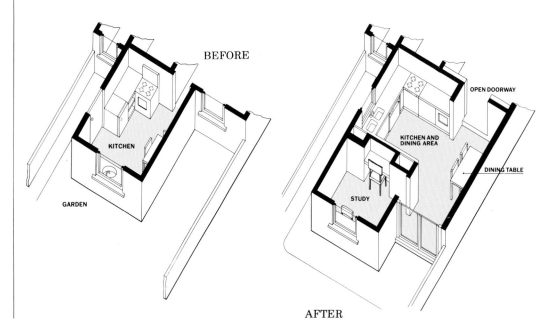

BEFORE

KITCHEN

GARDEN

OPEN DOORWAY

KITCHEN AND DINING AREA

DINING TABLE

STUDY

AFTER

WAYS WITH WINDOWS

Windows are obviously an important and integral part of a room's design and to replace them with frames which are out of character and proportion with the originals unbalances not only the room, but also the exterior of a home. That said, the number of window treatments available are numerous and suit all tastes, ranging from flounced frills to austere shutters. However, some windows are so inherently good-looking, especially some older designs, that they look best without any covering at all—weather and neighbours permitting.

This kind of bay window (above) can be seen in many a home, but here it has been dramatically altered by removing the architraves. The window frames are stripped back to the wood, apart from a thin beading strip which is painted black. Grey, stove enamelled metal bars are used as an outline and within their frame are painted marble-look panels. Roman blinds complete the crisp, uncluttered effect.

A window which isn't overlooked does not really need covering, except in winter to keep the room warm. Here (left) window space is used for storage; alternatively, the shelf could be filled with plants—a window sill of geraniums was traditionally the cottage dweller's answer to seeing all without being seen.

Stained glass windows (left) mask ugly views, afford privacy and cast delightful coloured light into a room. This sunflower design is particularly appealing because it gets away from the more formal static look of many a stained glass panel—you can almost feel the breeze which is blowing the flowers around. To fake stained glass see page 143.

This sumptuous look (left) is achieved with inexpensive fabric, but plenty of it. Translucent cotton voile is fully gathered along curtain poles and tied back in luxurious drapes—but really only for effect as patterned roller blinds are doing the work of keeping out the light and giving privacy.

Shutters (above) are an effective way of treating a window, as well as being good heat conservers and a security measure. Some old houses still retain theirs, but these are modern made-to-measure ones which have square cut-outs to match those of the table beneath.

DINING AND LIVING ROOMS

ALL LIT UP

BEFORE DINGY
HOME OFFICE

AFTER STYLISH
DINING ROOM

A small but very high and dark room (above) supplied unpromising material from which to make a welcoming dining room. The first requirement was to fill the obvious blank and replace the missing fireplace.

Looking out onto the well of a building, this old mansion flat room was a dingy, uninviting place and the previous owners had tried to compensate for lack of light with an uncompromising fluorescent tube across the ceiling. The tube was the first thing to go during redecoration and the present owner has relied instead on clever painting and other decorative effects to create a feeling of light and warmth. There was no fireplace, although there must have been once upon a time for the room looked incomplete without one, so he installed a polished metal Art Nouveau surround in an elongated style to complement the difficult, tall but narrow proportions of the room.

Initially the room was painted plain white, but this proved uninteresting so the owner added detail and colour. A dado rail was put in to match the one running along the hall; both dado and picture rails are useful for broadening out small rooms as well as breaking walls down into sections which can then be given different treatments: either paint or wallpaper, or a combination of both. Here the wall under the rail was painted to look like stone and stippled in 4-ft (1.3-m) 'blocks'. The wall above was given a complementary paint effect then coated with clear lacquer. The ceiling was left white to reflect the little available light and to match the woodwork.

At the window a thinly-slatted, silver Venetian blind masks the ugly view and may eventually be joined by plaid curtains to match the fabric on the Arts

A close-up view (above) of the paint techniques used in the completed dining room (right). Clever use of paint has 'warmed over' the room and the horizontal bands visually break down the overwhelming vertical lines to make the room appear larger.

and Crafts chairs, successfully teamed with an Aalto table. The room is otherwise too small to accommodate much more than this dining set and a sideboard for storage and serving. A poker-work, leather-framed mirror and a portrait of Sybil Thorndike above the mantelpiece successfully complete the furnishings and keep things simple, a necessity in such a limited space. The lighting is modern and beautifully plain, echoing the unadorned lines of the furnishings.

COLLECTOR'S PIECE

BEFORE
WINDOWLESS HALL/
RECEPTION AREA IN
AN OLD APARTMENT

AFTER BARONIAL
DINING ROOM

A dark room with four internal walls, the only window being one into another room (above) which neither gave much light nor looked good. The solution was to give the room dramatic artificial lighting and to mask the window with a decorative screen (above, right).

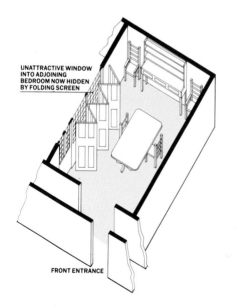

UNATTRACTIVE WINDOW
INTO ADJOINING
BEDROOM NOW HIDDEN
BY FOLDING SCREEN

FRONT ENTRANCE

Because it lacks any outside windows, this large hall was always going to be dark, no matter how it was decorated, so the owner decided to play up the fact and create a strongly dramatic room. A little light filtered in through the front door and from an ugly obscure-glassed window into an adjoining room; this eyesore is now hidden by a free-standing screen, an item not often seen in modern homes but one which is endlessly useful. This one is ingeniously made up from old wooden shutters and hung with an assortment of attractive china plates.

The first decorative step was to strip the floor; the embossed papered walls were also stripped and painted a dark glossy colour—which didn't work. The shine of the gloss only served to highlight the irregularities of the plaster—gloss

paint only looks good and gives a lacquer-like finish on perfect surfaces. The walls were repainted in eggshell (with a slight sheen) in a musky mushroom colour, as were the ceiling and the mouldings. The owner felt that brilliant white ceilings or mouldings picked out in white were too suburban. To do mouldings well, they should be picked out in various subtle colours as once was traditional. However, the ones in this room were not decorative enough to warrant such loving treatment and were painted instead to merge with the walls. It is true that the popularity of white paint on woodwork, mouldings and ceilings has been overworked; most of us automatically use unadulterated white when, with a little thought and imagination, other colours might be considered which would prove as successful and create more unusual and pleasing effects.

Visual interest was added to the large areas of blank wall in various, easy-to-copy ways. The skirting board was covered with a patterned wallpaper which, in turn, matches the fabric used to cover the narrow side tables made by the owner himself (see page 156). A kelim and a dhurrie hang behind each of these tables, their size helping to hide the uneven walls as well as acting as a suitable backdrop focusing attention on the tables. A collection of Thirties china from Britain covers the table tops, the dresser, screen and walls, giving the room an obvious theme and thus a strong identity which is best displayed against simple, classic furniture.

A carefully-arranged set piece (above). The fabric-covered table matches the wallpapered skirting board and a rug acts as a co-ordinating background to the overall display.

53

MIX AND MATCH

BEFORE TWO
ADJOINING BUT
SEPARATE ROOMS
IN A MANSION FLAT

AFTER COMBINED
LIVING/DINING
ROOM

A sparsely furnished room with dominating expanses of blank white wall (above) has been completely revamped by knocking through a well-proportioned opening (right). Adding colour to the surfaces picks out the architectural details. See next page for how the transformation was achieved.

The 'before' dining room (above) demonstrates a decorating fault common to many homes—the habit of painting radiators white, no matter what. This treatment serves to make them conspicuous; as they are not generally things of beauty they should be painted the same colour as the wall, so they merge with it and become as 'invisible' as possible (right). Venetian blinds visually extend the length of the windows and a good-sized mirror replaces the previous one, which was too small for its prominent position.

Two fair-sized rooms were turned into one large one (see previous page) by knocking out a section of the dividing wall between them and blocking up one of the two doorways into the hall. The owners were keen to make an elegantly proportioned opening, one which might always have been there since the apartment was built, so after working out its sizing, they carefully designed the frame which was ingeniously made up from a variety of different but readily-available standard mouldings and fittings. For instance, the corner section comprises a wooden drawer knob sawn flat at the back and inserted into a wooden curtain ring (see page 143 for an alternative). When all is covered over with paint, nobody can tell the difference. The handsome panelled doors were made-to-measure and given special hinges that allow the doors to fold back completely flat against the hall—which saves space.

The design for the double doorway is echoed in the two storage units in the dining area. The owners wanted these to look like pieces of furniture rather than fitted units and to create this effect designed them to stop short of the ceiling with the lower, closed sections jutting out in the style of classic free-standing bookcases. These were painted pale grey

to match the rest of the woodwork in the room (and in the whole apartment). But rather than use a paint technique to soften down and age the walls, a newly decorated look was avoided by wall-papering the walls with woodchip paper, the textured finish of which effectively softened down the pale pink.

Floorboards were sanded and sealed, and any damaged planks replaced by ones of the same age from the kitchen, which acted as a convenient source of flooring for the whole apartment before being given a brand new wooden floor in compensation. Natural wood is also featured in Venetian blinds and the large,

fold-out dining table teamed with inexpensive cane chairs (broken arms were renovated with strips of leather). Furnishings are a happy mixture of both old and modern; their common denominator, whether they be cane or chrome, being their strong simple shapes. Something to watch when mixing and matching furnishings is harmony of the textures, as well as shape and colour: pine and perspex can be the sort of combination to avoid. Finally, a mirror adds sparkle to the room—reflecting both light from the window and the movement of neighbouring treetops to the diners sitting opposite.

A balanced display of disparate objects makes this handsome fireplace (above) a strong focal point, with or without a blazing fire.

LIGHT RELIEF

BEFORE TWO
UPPER GROUND
FLOOR ROOMS

AFTER ONE
LARGE LIVING/DINING
ROOM LOOKING ON
TO THE GARDEN

The spaciousness required for the new room was created by knocking the two existing rooms into one, leaving as little evidence as possible of the dividing wall. The original sash window at the back of the house was set too high for the garden to be seen from a sitting position, so it was replaced by a pair of tall French windows which open inwards, visually extending the room into the garden. The windows were bought second-hand, which not only makes good economic sense, but their traditional design and proportions blend well with the style of the house.

A common problem when knocking two rooms into one is that you are usually left with two sentinel fireplaces, a constant reminder that the room was once divided. The solution here was to remove the least attractive one, re-using it elsewhere in the house, and treat the remaining plain, white-painted plaster one to a marblized finish (see page 152). As there was no budget to remove the redundant chimney breast, a shallow, glass-fronted cabinet was used to disguise it.

An all-over floor covering helps to unify a dual-purpose room. In this instance the owner did not want a fitted carpet, nor were the existing floorboards in good enough condition to sand and paint or varnish. She decided instead to invest in a new strip oak floor (see page 26).

The floor was expensive, but the final effect well worth it. Economies were made elsewhere, however, by not matching a cornice to the one already existing but instead, extending the picture rail around the new dining area. The rail was picked out in a bluey grey to match the windows and skirting boards; walls, ceilings and doors are a soft parchment.

The windows to the street have wooden Venetian blinds, while the French windows to the back garden are simply hung with cheap curtain lining material. The final touch—to make the room seem even more spacious—is the large old mirror placed between the two chimney breasts and opposite the hall doorway.

After the two old rooms were knocked into one (above), extra light was gained by replacing the high sash window with French windows. The newly-created rectangular room (right) is visually broadened with diagonally laid wood strip flooring.

The old table (top) is transformed with a variety of paint techniques (see page 150) which complement the intricacy of the rug on which it stands. The French windows to the back garden (above) are simply hung with cheap curtain lining material. Sewing tape is tacked to the fabric then tied in bows around old curtain rings.

HIGH TECH

BEFORE
BEDSITTING ROOM IN
A 1930s APARTMENT
BLOCK

AFTER HIGH
TECH COMBINED
DINING/LIVING/
BEDROOM

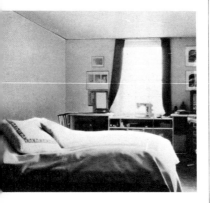

A very ordinary and uninspired room (above) was metamorphosed into an all-purpose, built-in living area (above right) where not an inch of space is wasted.

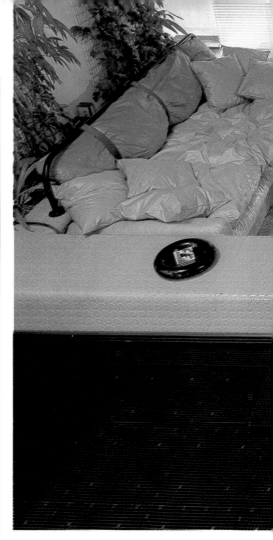

As an architect and designer of sleek, modern interiors, a cosy 1930s Tudor style apartment was an unlikely starting point for this owner, but she has skilfully covered up or disguised any hint of the original room. She moved in without a single piece of furniture and virtually everything in the room has been designed by her and built to specification; all has been done with much ingenuity and attention to detail. The starting point for the design was the green studded flooring offered to her at a price she couldn't refuse, and even though it is not the most easy colour to work with, she decided to use it. The same flooring has been used to cover the walls in her kitchen and bathroom (see page 122), but here it is continued only on to the low rectangular bench seating which also serves as a room divide: when the area is being used as a spare bedroom the vertical louvres are closed to give the sleeper privacy and passers-by access to the rest of the flat.

Flooring the walls

The walls of the room were in a bad state and rather than having them replastered—an expensive job—the owner disguised them with cheap vinyl flooring. The flooring contractors were bemused— but she now has easily maintained walls throughout the apartment which will last for longer than paint or wallpaper and always look immaculate. The only wall in the room not covered by flooring is the one facing the dining table. This is used as the apartment's main storage area and houses a run of mirror-fronted cupboards which visually double up the limited space of the room. The black mesh dining table hinges up against the wall where, when not needed, it looks like a black sculpture. It is made from industrial metal sheeting as are the matching multi-purpose stools which can also be used as side tables or even plant holders. For comfort, there are nautical cushions to sit on, and when these are not in use they also decorate the wall, along with a lifebelt. To a lover of boats, and their design, the nautical theme was a natural choice, not less because friends thought the blue carpeted sitting area resembled a swimming pool. The owner

had deliberately selected blue to tone down the green, continuing the blue carpet to cover the seating foam. On top of this are backrests made from duvets, for which she made the covers.

Wall grids above the seating act as anchorage for yellow plastic lights as well as a useful trellis for plants. The radiators are conventional models disguised with metal vents (cut to size at a builders' merchants) which are hung in front of them on red butcher's hooks. The vents are almost an exact match for the thin louvre blinds at the window above. Finally, the flooring is at last used for what it was originally designed. Open-tread black plastic squares were cheap and just as easy to vacuum as carpeting. The whole apartment shows what can be done in a small space on a budget, illustrating that with imagination you can use all sorts of familiar items in unexpected and original places.

The room ready for dining (left). The table folds away when not in use. For sleeping, the vertical blinds can screen off the seating units which transform into bed and duvets (below).

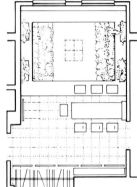

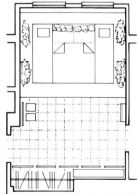

A run of mirror-fronted cupboards (left) adds extra visual space and light. The dining table is hinged back against the wall until needed.

STUDIED SERENITY

BEFORE BASIC ROOM WITH UGLY ALCOVES

AFTER SOPHISTICATED LIVING ROOM

A simple, stylishly classic room is what this owner was striving for. Her main aim was to achieve a fake Mediterranean light—not an easy thing to do in London—and she chose an airy colour scheme of white, pale grey and blue. Enlivening touches of red are subtly but deliberately added here and there: in a display of fruit, a magazine cover, even in the flowers on the outside window sill, which proves that colour schemes need not be restricted to large furnishing items.

Many metres of inexpensive thin white cotton are the key to this room's transformation: French pleated, it is hung at the windows, in front of the alcoves and in front of the counter into the kitchen (out of shot) so the galley is hidden from view. To add a touch of drama to the windows, extra fabric was swathed across the dull brass rods (replacements for the previous white ones) and the curtains are always kept closed, their thinness allowing light to filter through and successfully create the intended impression of a sunny clime outside. The hanging fabric is a simple disguise solution to ugly fittings, bad walls or unattractive windows: the fabric can be easily taken down for washing or removed altogether when dirty or when the occupant moves home.

The two day-beds were knocked together by the owner, who has only a basic knowledge of woodworking skills. (Anyone with less confidence could check out their local second-hand shop or contact a carpenter.) Their tapered leg style was influenced by a French empire day-bed featured in a magazine and their upholstery comprises Japanese mattresses (futons) laid on top and covered with striped mattress ticking; there are striped bolsters and cushions (also home-made) to match. Mattress ticking, cotton duck, canvas, and lining materials are all inexpensive fabrics which always look good provided you don't skimp on the

amount: the cheaper the material, the more you should use, especially with curtains. The day-bed bases are 'washed' with paint; one thin coat of paint applied so that the grain of the wood shows through. This method is a great labour-saving device, employing one coat of paint rather than four (primer, under-coat, two top coats) and will appeal to the reluctant decorator.

Both the coffee table and the dining table (out of picture) were self-made, the latter draped with an old and exquisite white Swiss lace cloth. The whole room is studied and serene, thanks to clever use of colour and classically inspired furnishings; objects are isolated so that they have room to breathe and be seen and any clutter is avoided. It is also the perfect foil for the owner's work (all the pots are designed and decorated by her as well as the paintings and silkthrow) which is just as well as it is her showroom as well as living room.

IDEAS UNLIMITED

BEFORE LIVING ROOM, INAPPROPRIATELY DECORATED AND FURNISHED

AFTER STYLISH AND COMFORTABLE LARGE LIVING ROOM/STUDY

This large room was once an artists' studio and consequently its high-set windows face north to catch the best light. When its present owner (an architect and interior designer) took it over she considered its height and light long and hard before beginning redecoration. The previous owners would have done well to do the same thing: their low-backed seating, small scale furniture and colours were completely out of keeping with the room and dwarfed by its scale.

First job for the new owner was to replace the large, old radiators which were boxed-in under the windows. Modern flat radiators were substituted so that they could be concealed with pieces of furniture; others were incorporated at the bottom of the tall book-shelves which were specially made to order. These are of a simple design, with tops made up from different sizes of standard mouldings joined together. If the height of the bookcases needs to be raised to accommodate more shelves, the top can simply be lifted off and re-added. The insides of the shelves are painted a dark colour to give the structures a more solid appearance—a useful visual trick. The radiators they conceal are disguised with chicken wire stretched across a frame which looks surprisingly chic and also lets the warm air out.

How not to furnish a room with a high ceiling (far left). The furniture is too small and bitty, making the room all fuss to shoulder height with acres of nothingness above.

Vast areas of empty wall space are transformed by balanced and built-up arrangements such as the one above. It is important that the furnishings are visually linked with the paintings.

Bookcases (left), scaled to correspond to the room's height, stand sentinel to the replacement fireplace: combined with the central painting they form a balanced and strong arrangement. Sofas are also on a larger than average scale. Colours and patterns are warm and inviting—very necessary in a north-facing room.

In the 'before' living room (right), pictures float forlornly in a sea of wall. After redesigning (above), bookcases fill the end wall almost entirely and yet their contents serve to break up the space and add visual interest. A desk is given extra prominence with a homemade felt screen which also serves as a pin-board.

The previous fireplace was ripped out and replaced with a stunning marble one but not before extra depth was added to the area so that the fireplace gained more prominence. The two sofas were made to measure for the room and consequently made on a larger than average scale so that they do not look lost in such a generously sized room. The rest of the furniture came from an 'ordinary' sized house and various clever ploys were needed to increase its visual importance amongst such vastness. A side table holds a giant birdcage (with imitation birds), two tall plants rise upwards and a

How to transform a round chipboard table (left). A plate of pebbles, a pile of pictures and a vase of fresh greenery make an impressive tablescape.

Plain old chicken-wire masks the radiators installed under the bookcases (above) but also lets out the heat.

painting boldly filling the wallspace takes the eye up further. The desk was made to look more important with a small folding screen which the owner made from felt and blockboard; as well as raising the visual height of the desk, it acts as a useful personal pinboard. The tall trolley beside the desk also helps to add weight and importance. The library table in the middle of the room with its dome of stuffed birds is a suitably dominant eye-catcher and not only fills an awkward space but serves to divide the room into its two different purposes. Large pictures also help to fill up the extensive wall area.

The overall effect of the room is rich in warm colours and comfortable textures; it also reveals clever tricks to copy. Lampshades covered with colour cut-outs are darkly varnished to look like authentic Victorian decoupage; a chenille bedspread is thrown over a makeshift chipboard table; silk flowers painted to more subtle and sophisticated colours nestle among real flowers; folding captains' chairs have been 're-covered' with interlaced rows of upholstery webbing; interesting baskets, tins, cutlery trays and so on are used as alternative cachepots and ashtrays.

ASTRO HOME

BEFORE DULL AND FEATURELESS ROOM

AFTER VIBRANT, SUNNY, LIVING ROOM

The biggest decision faced by the new owners of this room was whether they could face living with the hacienda-style arch installed by the previous occupant when two rooms had been knocked through into one large one. They decided that the mess and inconvenience of altering its curved shape into something more sympathetic with the architecture of the house (Edwardian) or else removing it altogether (which would have involved installing a support beam) was more than they could bear and let it be. It was a choice that worked out well for them, but is not always a wise dictate to follow. If a new home has a prominent feature you don't like, it is sometimes wiser to alter it at once than let it irk you for years afterwards. What they did feel prepared to deal with, however, was the arch knocked into the chimney breast, which was squared off and now houses a smart Thirties-style drinks trolley. The chimney breast in the other room displayed a particularly unlovely crescent-shaped brick fireplace, so this was removed and plastered over. It is always a problem to know what to do with a chimney breast after a fireplace has been removed: page 74 offers some useful alternatives.

The tiled walls are an illusion to avoid the work and expense of ceramic tiling; laminate board imitating the real thing was used instead, also serving as an excellent camouflage for badly pitted walls. The board runs continuously along one wall from the front to the back of the house.

The sunny yellow colour scheme is actually a second choice for the room. Originally the owners teamed the pale grey with terracotta, to match their terracotta metal furniture and covers; but after a while this combination was felt to be too dark and heavy, so walls and ceiling were treated to a textured look with two shades of dabbed-on yellow paint to brighten things up. (Textured

Two rooms already knocked into one by the previous owners present an odd mixture of different architectural styles (above).

finishes are also an ideal way of playing down cracked or uneven walls.) The metal furniture was resprayed with a hammer-look finish metallic grey paint and the cushions recovered with a yellow/grey print to complete the vibrant effect.

The lighting was also altered.

Avoiding further serious structural changes, the rooms are unified and given an up-to-date look (left) by means of a strong colour scheme. All-metal furniture is used throughout which also helps to unite the room. A Venetian blind partially obscures the—as yet—unlovely view of the backyard.

Previously there had been a track with spotlights, but these were too bright and were replaced with wall-mounted uplighters. Existing bulkhead lights were retained but painted yellow to match the scheme. Lighting can make or break a room and should be given the same consideration as any other decorative feature; spotlights badly handled can be as deadening to a room's atmosphere as the ubiquitous single central ceiling light.

Finally the pale, grey carpet, Venetian blinds and shiny steel shelving are suitably neutral enough to fit in with any other colour change the owners might want to try in the years to come.

69

CALM AND COLLECTED

BEFORE SIXTIES-STYLE KNOTTY PINE

AFTER EIGHTIES-STYLE GREY-PAINTED CALM

This small home had been given the full Scandinavian Sixties treatment by its previous owners and was more like a sauna than a living room. The new occupants found the knotty-pine-everywhere look overwhelmingly difficult to live with and while stripping the wood of its harsh coating of shiny lacquer would have toned it down to a softer, bleached hue, it would have required far too many extra hours of work. The owners opted instead for painting the wood, which did seem a bit like sacrilege to them at first, but the end result proved them wrong. With a colour scheme based on pale blue and pale grey, the room has completely 'calmed down' and creates a far more serene atmosphere.

The walls are grey, with skirting board, door frame and so on painted to match, which helps them merge rather than stand out. Painting everything the same colour in this way makes a room appear larger; picking out the woodwork in white would have broken up the space and looked more fussy. It is also a mistake to draw attention to any ugly skirting boards or other not particularly attractive features by painting them a contrasting colour: much better to resort to disguise by painting them the same colour as the walls so they disappear. This same principle was applied to the brick fireplace which the owners wanted to change to something more architecturally sympathetic. But for the time being they have been happy to paint it grey and pep it up with smart black ceramic tiles to cover the hearth terrazzo. Slate would have been equally effective.

The ceiling is painted a paler tone of grey than the walls to avoid any

The fascinating sort of transformation a few pots of paint can achieve is shown far left and left. Even without the finishing touch of new furnishings, the room has not only changed character but proportion as well.

oppressive feeling and the staircase picked out in a pretty pale blue. The treads were left natural pine to provide a visual link with the floor, but were partially covered with pieces of blue rubber matting to soften the staircase's dominant lines. It also provides a practical non-slip surface—essential with children around.

Furnishings continue the pale blue and grey theme—again a good ploy in a small room for it means that furniture, especially large items such as sofas, don't dominate the space as they would if they were in contrasting colours. Patterned dhurries soften the floor and add a feeling of warmth and comfort as well as that vital contrast of pattern and texture—without them the room would be too monochromatic; a fitted patterned carpet would also have worked well in this context. Two interesting large plants (more effective here than a selection of smaller ones dotted around) counteract the room's fairly austere lines and add an alternative dash of life and colour.

BRIGHT ARRAY

BEFORE TWO
FIRST-FLOOR
BEDROOMS

AFTER OPEN-
PLAN LIVING ROOM

The view from this home is one of its main assets, but the previous owners had done little to exploit it. The first floor—which offers the best vista, and a balcony—had been divided between two bedrooms and was consequently unused all day, which seemed a terrible waste. The new occupant put paid to this state of affairs by bringing the living room upstairs and opening out the whole area. The hall wall and dividing wall of the rooms were knocked out to create one large, bright and airy room through which light streams from windows at both ends. In order not to detract from this effect or from the view, no curtains or blinds cover the windows by day or night; instead, some inexpensive cotton is draped casually around the main window frame to soften its outline (the material in itself is thin enough to allow light to filter through). The house is not overlooked so there is no problem with privacy.

The room was renovated so that as many period details as possible were kept. Cornices damaged while walls were being knocked out were replaced by a craftsman (but alternatively there is always the ready-made, off-the-peg variety) and the much painted-over and boarded-up fireplace was carefully restored to its original magnificent slate and flowered-tile state. Walls are white, woodwork grey and the floor sanded and sealed. This soothing and neutral back-

The photograph above shows a room with its basic structural and decorating work complete and with only the all-important finishing touches to go. Furnishings cheer the room (right), instantly making it more cosy and less austere.

ground enhances the room's dimensions and looks cool and calm in summer, but in winter can be somewhat cold and unwelcoming. Therefore at that time of year extra colour and cosiness is added by additional furnishings, especially rugs, which are flung over the sofas as well as the floor. There is no reason why a room should not be dressed in winter and summer 'clothes', just as we are.

The original layout of this terraced house reveals a conventional first floor: two rooms and a staircase (right). The bedroom walls and hall were knocked out and the area transformed into one large living room.

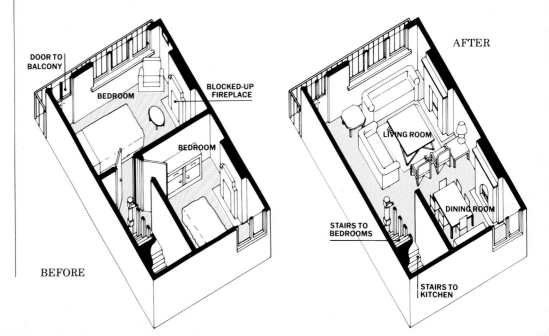

DOOR TO
BALCONY

BEDROOM

BLOCKED-UP
FIREPLACE

BEDROOM

BEFORE

AFTER

LIVING ROOM

DINING ROOM

STAIRS TO
BEDROOMS

STAIRS TO
KITCHEN

IDEAS FOR FIREPLACES

A fireplace containing a cheery fire undoubtedly provides the natural focal point of any room. It is when the fire is not burning that the fireplace needs special attention, for an empty grate looks rather bleak and needs some kind of decorative device to add interest. Alternatively, if the fireplace has been removed but the chimney breast remains, there are many interesting ways the space can be utilized other than replacing the fireplace. In a kitchen, for instance, it could be used as a built-in barbecue with ready-made ventilation, or in a children's room as a dolls' house.

Kitchen chimney breasts which no longer have fireplaces may be treated in various ways. Here (left) the chimney breast is used to house an Aga and the area above it has been fitted with open shelves filled with decorative items to make it into a focal point.

A clever idea for utilizing a redundant fireplace (right). This empty space in a children's bedroom was ingeniously transformed into a dolls' house. For step-by-step instructions as to how it was done, see page 144.

Stylish simplicity shows what can be done with a fireplace when it is not host to a roaring fire (right). Dried flowers and herbs hang from a knotted rope and look particularly effective. Above the mantel, a dark picture with an appropriate food theme balances the dark grate area of this kitchen fireplace.

Fireplaces need not be painted all one colour. This one (right) emphasizes its mouldings by using two colours. Alternatively, marble, tortiseshell, or any other special paint technique will transform a dull surround.

The design of this kitchen chimney breast (left) is straightforward and uncluttered: a surround of white tiles, a white tiled shelf which holds a mini-oven and a shiny chrome rail for tea towels and oven gloves.

OPEN LIVING

A wide open loft space (above) is divided into distinctly private and public areas, separated from each other by an angled wall of clear and frosted glass. The public side (left and right) is a harmonious blend of soft colour and hard angles.

STREET WISE

BEFORE OPEN
LOFTSPACE

AFTER OPEN
AND PRIVATE
LIVING SPACES

The basic space was an open loft with a central skylight, corner bathroom and a main wall of north-facing windows. The architects were asked by the owners to turn it into a combination of one large living space for cooking, dining, sitting and working as well as two bedrooms, bathroom and laundry. How the architects accomplished this myriad of spaces—all daylit—was by dividing the apartment into public and private areas with a wall of clear and frosted glass as the division, the frosted glass providing privacy where needed. Although simple in concept, this gridded glass wall cleverly incorporates kitchen cupboards, doorways (conventional double doors as well as a large rotating panel), ventilation panels and also top windows for letting light into the rooms beyond.

The inspiration for the exact and unusual slanting position of the glass wall and the rooms was the New York City street grid: the rooms are 'buildings' and the corridors 'streets' which open out into the large room, 'the piazza'. The 'buildings' are painted different colours in restfully soft shades and gradually step down in size to give added perspective as well as automatically leading the eye out of the large windows and towards the city beyond. The furniture has been arranged to reinforce this progression, by being carefully placed and kept to a minimum—with so much architectural interest, busy furnishings would have been too much. Kitchen clutter and a communications post (which houses entry-phone, television and so on) are both hidden from the general seating area with partition walls of varying heights.

FADED GLORY

BEFORE OLD
HANDBAG WORKSHOP

AFTER COMBINED
LIVING ROOM
AND KITCHEN

A disused old factory with spartan architectural charm—particularly evident in the beamed and boarded roof (above and right)—was inexpensively turned into an open-plan living room/kitchen with a minimum of structural and decorative change.

Erected by the suffragettes as a toy factory, then later converted in the Thirties into a handbag factory and engineering firm, this building provided an unusual shell from which to make a home. The living room and kitchen shown here are upstairs in the most spectacular part of the building where the architect owner carried out as little alteration work as possible to preserve its uniqueness. All that was done structurally was to remove the recent partitions and to replace one of the Thirties metal frame windows with a set of specially made French windows in the same style. Now when sitting down it is possible to see out into the garden: the room has been visually opened out by

this change to feel even more spacious. When replacing windows like this, it is always best to try to keep the new ones sympathetic to the architecture of the building both in proportion, and, if possible, in design.

Walls, beams and the wooden ceiling were left virtually as they were found, their faded and peeling surfaces simply brushed down to remove loose flakes of old paint, then left in distressed splendour; this authentic aged effect would be hard, exhausting, but not totally impossible to emulate. Such an architecturally unusual room needed no further embellishment. In contrast, the bedroom downstairs was undistinguished, and so the owner decided to give

Assorted belongings of mixed heritage make for an idiosyncratic display (above). Chairs which once graced a ladies' hairdressing salon and inexpensive cotton sheeting both frame new French doors specially made to match existing windows (left).

it hard, glossy and mirror-smooth newly painted walls.

Old-fashioned cast iron radiators to suit the ambience of the room upstairs were found secondhand and installed. Although their rust was first brushed off, they too were left unpainted. In fact so many people have been renovating old houses that a few manufacturers have responded and it is now possible to buy brand new, old-style radiators.

The room's furnishings demonstrate how an original and stylish effect can be achieved in a very inexpensive way. The drapes at the window are simply metres of cotton sheeting, unhemmed, pinch pleated and held tight between two poles. These are supported by coat hooks onto which the fabric is draped. Furniture comprises two armchairs saved from a skip, chromed chairs from a ladies' hairdresser, and a hammock. The fridge is secondhand, also the plans chest which has been adapted to form a desk and china display arrangement. The cheap kitchen units were given a certain panache by marbling with paint to match the plastered breeze block wall behind. Clip-on spotlights highlight and enhance the beamed ceiling—authentic dried out damp patches and all.

OUTSIDE IN

BEFORE SMALL BACK YARD

AFTER GARDEN ROOM AND TERRACE

DOOR MADE FROM WINDOW

NEW TERRACE

STAIRCASE DOUBLES AS LARDER-ENTRANCE FROM KITCHEN

GARDEN ROOM

KITCHEN EXTENDED AND DOORS ADDED

The back of a terraced house was transformed by the addition of an upstairs balcony, sets of French windows and an indoor/outdoor glassed garden room. Sunshine and greenery over-spill into the house via these and newly-created mirrored skylights.

This extension has been handled with careful thought and planning, the owners resisting the ease of simply adding on a box-shaped structure which bears no architectural relevance to the existing building (a 19th-century terraced town house). The garden room, which also acts as the laundry room, opens out entirely when the doors are folded back, or can be made private by closing doors and drawing blinds on the roof and sides. Quarry tiles have been used to pave the garden, the conservatory and the kitchen beyond it so there is no visual 'break' between house and garden, so encouraging the feeling that the interior continues naturally outside. The garden room was designed and constructed from components made by three separate companies but the same effect could equally well be achieved by using a cheaper, prefabricated type of conservatory/greenhouse.

Garden terraces

The transformed back yard originally measured 6 m × 9 m (20 ft × 30 ft) By extending the kitchen a roof terrace was created, making up for the space lost in the garden below which is now reduced to 6 m (20 ft). The terrace is paved with lightweight terracotta-coloured concrete tiles and contains two skylights which open down into the house; their interior vertical sides are mirrored so that extra light and the potted greenery along the terrace are reflected into the kitchen below.

The concrete stairs from the balcony are covered with engineering bricks and provide useful storage space underneath in the form of a cool larder: access is from the kitchen. A prefabricated staircase could just as well have been purchased and substituted here instead, as a less expensive alternative.

The remaining strip of garden, out of shot in this photograph, is in stepped bricked terraces out of which have been created a series of various flower beds and a small pond. It is an ideal arrangement for anyone looking for an easily maintained garden, efficient and functional yet maintaining charm and character.

SCHOLASTIC BRILLIANCE

BEFORE OLD, ONE-ROOMED COUNTRY CHURCH SCHOOL HOUSE

AFTER OPEN-PLAN MULTI-PURPOSE SPACE, STILL IN TRANSITION

A barren school room (above) initially had only its size to commend it as a possible home.

A spartan but large school hall with a lowered fake ceiling, good sized windows and a wooden floor: these were the bare bones from which this comfortable home was created. First to go was the false ceiling, which was ripped out to reveal a high, pitched roof leaving plenty of space to build a sleeping platform at the windowless end of the room. Not yet finished—the balustrading will be painted off-white—it has a beautiful old French oak staircase for access and the bed itself is an extravagantly draped faked four poster. Behind the bed is the clothes storage, hidden from downstairs visitors by a moon and stars painted screen—a simple alternative to the ubiquitous row of fitted cupboards.

The focal point of the main room is the fireplace, created out of nothing by bits and pieces: scrolled pillars brought back from Portugal, a top supplied by the builder, local flagstones as a hearth, and fake Delft tiles painted by the owner himself and copied roughly from a book. To age the newness of the chimney breast's interior he used a thin wash of paint which soaked into the concrete.

As well as being an interior decorator, the owner is an expert at different paint techniques, many of which are displayed in the room and show what can be achieved quite inexpensively with time, skill and practice. At present he is decorating the walls with a stencil he designed and cut himself (the wall above the fireplace is yet to be treated), using a technique which is fast and furious and not at all painstaking. He believes the charm of stencilling is in its roughness (see page 148) and that it should not present a neat pristine finish. However, his walls *are* professionally finished off with a containing blue band of border. To break up the vast expanse of wall he painted the dado beneath the chair rail a plain colour, having first lowered the rail (which is to be marbled) a foot or so from its original position because it was not proportionally correct for the room.

The floor is also all his own work, copied from a similar one in a book of Italian interiors and is the sort of design which only works well in large spaces. Simple to do (see page 147), the thinness of the paint allows the wood grain to show through although eventually the central white squares will be marbled. The painted Gothic style table in the background is also his own handiwork; it started life as a plain stripped pine kitchen table.

By removing the false ceiling enough height was gained to instal a sleeping platform (left). A grand fireplace —literally made up from bits and pieces—acts as the room's lynchpin.

Candles add theatrical drama to any room and this one is no exception; although the tin candelabra are only lit on high days and holidays they add to the comfortable, lived-in atmosphere of the room. Out of sight are the two other tiny rooms of the house: the children's cloakroom is now the bathroom and the school kitchen has been converted to a domestic one. The outside lavatories are destined for transformation into the guest bedroom—one day.

Fancy fingerwork with the paintbrush saves on buying tiles (above) and flooring (left, see page 147).

PERIOD PIECE

BEFORE EMPTY
SPACE IN A RIVERSIDE
WAREHOUSE

AFTER ARTS AND
CRAFTS-INSPIRED
OPEN LIVING SPACE

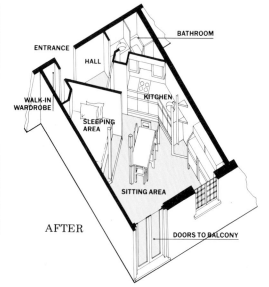

ENTRANCE

BATHROOM

HALL

WALK-IN
WARDROBE

KITCHEN

SLEEPING
AREA

SITTING AREA

AFTER

DOORS TO BALCONY

As fans and collectors of furniture from the Arts and Crafts movement (which flourished in England in the second half of the 19th century), the owners of this apartment and their architect took this period as their theme. What they wanted was not a reproduction of the era, but a modern interpretation of it. A diamond pattern on the underside of the dining table was used as a recurring motif and a basis for the living space layout which consequently has angled partition walls to form the main room, lobby, walk-in clothes closet and bathroom.

Fixtures and fittings throughout are oak. The new skirting boards and unusual wooden cornices, which have concealed lighting, both have the diamond motif grouted along them, as do the kitchen units. In some instances the diamonds have been filled with coloured glass and are illuminated from behind. Wherever possible, the kitchen units conceal the modern appliances—even the control panel of the built-in cooker folds away separately. (The chrome tap is a temporary measure to be soon replaced by something less obtrusive.) The working surface is made up of small white mosaics (again, the diamond shape) which match up to those in the bathroom (see page 127). Vertical beams delineate the cooking and the sleeping areas. The latter is provided with drawer storage space under the bed; above it is a coloured, old glass panel which is illuminated from the clothes closet, access to which is from the hall. Around the bed, as in other areas of the room, there is plenty of shelf space. It is a necessary requisite to display, without crowding, the many pieces of the owners' Arts and Crafts pottery and pewter pieces, as well as examples of their own work.

Matching materials

The other common materials in use throughout the area are wired glass and ironwork. The handsome, specially-designed double doors into the living area and the kitchen units are given this treatment, and the main iron columns which were once white-painted have been matched to the new ironwork with a coat of black paint and then a covering of stove-black which has been burnished to a mellow sheen. The floor is cork, each tile carefully hand-tinted with thinned artist's oils and then varnished for protection. In harmony with all these shades of earthy colours, and offsetting them, are richly patterned rugs and bed-coverings.

Out of sight in the photograph is the general seating area, neatly and compactly planned for such a small apartment. From it a pair of double doors leads out onto a small balcony, reminiscent of a boat deck on a luxury liner—and not altogether inappropriate since the balcony overlooks a canal that leads to the river.

Intricately manoeuvred in a small, bare space (below, far left) an apartment full of Arts and Crafts references (left and below). Concealed lights throw into relief the original beams and the new wooden cornice, complete with diamond motifs.

FIRST-FLOOR FREEDOM

BEFORE TWO ROOMS AND A STAIRWAY

AFTER ONE LARGE FIRST-FLOOR LIVING ROOM

The first floor landing (above) presented a conventional appearance and layout until all the dividing walls were knocked out (right and far right), plus a section of ceiling (far right). A darkly-stained floor is less common-place than the more usual stripped pine treatment.

The owner of this house chose to have his living room on the first floor rather than at ground level partly because he dislikes having to use curtains, but mainly because being situated above street level means that views are more open and there is less likelihood of being overlooked. An airy, open space was required and not only was the wall between the two rooms knocked down, but also the one onto the stairway. Stairs now come directly into the room.

Not content with this, he also knocked out the ceiling above the bay window so that the rafters—which were linseed oiled—are exposed and there is a vista up to roof height. The room upstairs is a bedroom and with a third of its floor gone it is possible to look down from it into the living room. Brass safety rails and a succession of roller blinds provide safety and privacy when needed. The remainder of the living room ceiling was boarded over and painted the same pale green as the walls.

The final structural alteration involved turning a back sash window into French doors which lead out onto a newly-created roof terrace. The main wall of the room was stripped of plaster and the exposed brickwork given four coats of marine varnish, while the floor was sanded and stained mahogany.

It is an atmospheric room with a motley collection of furnishings that include a cable spool coffee table and an 18th century chest which houses a stereo. The success of this conversion lies mainly in the creation of broadened horizons—both upwards as well as sideways.

VERTICAL VISION

BEFORE FOUR TINY BEDROOMS ON TWO TOP FLOORS

AFTER OPEN-PLAN LIVING ROOM, BATHROOM AND SLEEPING GALLERY

SKYLIGHT

CEILING REMOVED

TRAP DOORS

PART OF FLOOR REMOVED

GLASS ENCASED STAIRCASE TO KITCHEN

The wedge-shape of this house is very unusual, but the conversion of two floors into open-plan living space would be equally well suited to a more conventionally-shaped home. So small were the original four bedrooms that anyone standing in the middle of one could touch both the chimney breast and the wall opposite to it. In fact the combined floor-space taken up by the chimney breasts was considerable, so all were removed and the pleasure of having an open fire sacrificed. The hall walls were also dispensed with so that staircases would lead straight into rooms.

The lower of the two floors is now the general living area and to prevent all the warm air and cooking smells rising into it from the kitchen/dining room below, the staircase opening is boxed-in, but with glass, so that the room is still opened out visually. The original old staircases were kept, both because they were attractive to look at (their pleasing rounded bottom steps contrasted well with all the straight lines elsewhere), and also because their positioning could not have been improved. In the photograph on the left, the staircase is yet to be painted.

Open and shut
The idea for the roof-light and trap doors came to the architect owner when the house was in a state of dereliction. During renovation the building had to be gutted, and while the roof was off he looked up from the basement to the sky. It struck him that this sort of vertical vista would be worth keeping when the house was habitable, and the idea was incorporated into the new scheme. The trap doors can be shut when privacy or working space is needed, but they usually remain open, creating a kind of gallery effect on the top floor.

At the narrow end of the gallery floor is a newly-built bathroom above which plenty of head height has been left to fit in a sleeping platform. Because the back yard is so tiny, the 'garden' has virtually been brought inside with a plethora of plants round the outside of the bathroom and gallery. The effect of these, combined with all the skylights and windows, is akin to a conservatory.

Decoration has been kept simple. All the walls are white, the windows are stripped back to bare wood and the floor, which once graced a school gym, is mahogany. Furnishings are also simple, leaving the conversion's interesting shapes and prospects as the focus of attention. Even though the house has been totally rebuilt inside, it maintains its essential character; this is something which very many insensitive conversions obliterate—though much to their detriment.

A terraced house opened out not only horizontally, but vertically as well (far left). The upward vista is increased by a large skylight.
Trap doors (above) can be shut if privacy is required on the bathroom/bedroom floor; otherwise the view is kept open.

DECORATIVE FURNITURE

For those who prefer to scour secondhand shops for unusual furnishing buys rather than shop for them brand new, there are various ways and means of pepping up purchases which may be a little damaged, or else perfectly sound but lacking real originality. The same applies to furniture already in existence at home which may have been bought some time ago, but now needs a facelift. Paint and fabric pieces used imaginatively can achieve miraculous transformations.

Furniture which has been painted with dash and exuberance. Page 149 shows how to emulate such colourful dashes.

A junk shop purchase transformed with various paint techniques (right). Remember, it is a waste of time to spend hours painting up a piece of furniture which is basically rickety, unsound or an ugly shape, so choose and restore your junk shop piece carefully.

A junk shop wardrobe (right) handsome in its own way, but too large to fit into the room concerned. Virtually cut in two and rejoined into a triangular shape, it is now installed as a linen and toiletry cupboard in a bathroom (above). For instructions on how to do something similar, see page 144.

A badly-marked, pale-coloured sofa is given a new lease of life with knotted sheets and a bank of co-ordinating cushions (above). Draping an armchair or a sofa can look just as effective. Use shawls or rugs, lengths of fabric, or, as here, something borrowed from the linen cupboard.

Who said that sofas should be the same colour all over? This one (left) has a coat of many colours which alters a basic shape into something a bit more interesting, especially if you don't like scatter cushions. Note how the cover colours are picked up in the rug and the painting.

HALLS AND STAIRCASES

SPIRALLING METAL

BEFORE SINGLE-STOREY LOFT ROOM

AFTER DOUBLE-HEIGHT ROOM WITH SPIRAL STAIRCASE

A spiralling staircase leads up to a platform which was created by removing the original ceiling of the room.

The focal point of this conversion (right), which involved taking out the ceiling to make a double-height room, is the beautiful blue curving staircase and balustrading. Made to order and designed by the architect, it was kept as visually light and delicate as possible and outshines the usually more stolid-looking spiral staircases which can be bought pre-fabricated. The diameter of this staircase is also larger than the norm, which means that going up and down is not the trial it can be with many curving stairways. It was supplied by a metal-ware company which normally manufactures fire escapes, steel beams and the like.

Yellow mesh
The yellow-painted metal staircase (far right) was also built to architect specifications, but this time is a squared-off half spiral. Painted a brilliant yellow, its natural wood treads match the living room floor and its structure is safely encased with wire mesh panels which prevent it from looking too heavy or dominant. A similar look, but smaller in scale, is featured on page 137 as a stairway to a bunk bed.

Generally speaking, a spiral staircase is the most space-saving of designs, but remember that with some it is possible to manoeuvre up and down only the smallest pieces of furniture.

All sorts of ready-made designs are on the market, from fancy Victorian ironwork types to simpler, more modern affairs.

The grid of this made-to-measure staircase matches that of the tiles on the custom-built central stove.

STAIRS AS STORAGE

BEFORE OLD STAIRCASE INTO A BASEMENT

AFTER MODERN STAIRCASE WITH TOY STORAGE FOR A NEWLY-CREATED PLAYROOM

A rickety flight of stairs (above) was not worth saving and so was replaced with a made-to-measure design that is sturdy enough to double as a climbing frame.

*Three ways of going up
and down at home
(above, left and far left).
A far cry from conven-
tional stairs, these have
the added advantage of
supplying storage
in a usually wasted
space.*

The area under a staircase is a useful spot for utilizing as extra storage space, or even, in some cases, as an extra room such as a small cloakroom or bedsit kitchen. In this instance (left) the old staircase was in need of replacement and a new design was installed to incorporate an attractive and substantial safety rail which also doubles as a climbing frame for children. Underneath the treads is a considerable amount of storage space which can be hidden behind doors that are painted to provide blackboards, or alternatively left open to display colourful toys. Practical rubber studded flooring in cheery red is used on the stairs as well as the ground. A similar openshelved staircase can be seen in a bedroom on page 134.

The clean-lined staircase (above) is really more of a sculptural than a practical affair as it leads only to a tiny landing and is more a means of access to watering the plants. Its main function is to act as a large cupboard, with flushfronted doors designed to be as unobtrusive as possible and which open to a light touch.

An entrance hall and staircase (above, right) have been saved from dullness by a decoration scheme which uses strong, bright colour and rigid symmetry. Curved bottom steps are flanked by red cubes which could possibly be used for storing telephone directories and/or outdoor footwear such as Wellington boots. Further storage space is hidden away in the walls of the stairway.

COUNTRY HOUSE STYLE

BEFORE FUSSY, UNCO-ORDINATED HALL

AFTER STYLISH HALL WITH STRONG CHARACTER

The hall above presented a confusing jumble of levels and doors. These were simplified and French windows substituted for a sash one. A strong, muted colour now throws the interesting architectural details into relief (right) and makes for a bolder and more definite effect than a lighter colour, or pattern, would have done.

The first step with this hall was to improve it architecturally: the door half-way along the landing was removed, so was the partition, and the ordinary sash window changed for French doors which now lead out onto a newly-created roof terrace. The floor area was levelled and expanded space, new spindles and newel available landing (specially strengthened to take the weight) and to outline the expanded space, new spindles and newel posts were made up to match with the old. The rafters were then covered over and the ceiling plastered. These alterations drastically changed the character of the hall even before decorating: it is always worth considering ways in which a room can be improved structurally to gain space, vistas or whatever, before reaching for the paint brush.

As this hall gets plenty of light (there is a skylight above the stairs and open doorways into various rooms) the architect owner chose a subtle but darkish colour, with the woodwork picked out in a specially mixed off-white/beige colour. The paint is matt finish throughout as gloss paint would certainly have been overwhelmingly shiny on this amount of woodwork. The carpet is a light neutral shade, counteracting the darker walls.

The hall is simply and effectively furnished. There is a garden bench in the style of Chatsworth—one of England's loveliest stately homes—with a mattress added for comfort. This has been covered in a cheap fabric, although the piping was expensive (the same principle has been applied to the curtains and is the professional's way of achieving a stylish look for less money). The rows of prints are taken from a book and framed, and an overflowing basket of dried hydrangeas on top of a humble block-board table hidden from view by draped floor-length cloths reinforces the country house style.

PAINTED PASSAGES

BEFORE
PARTITIONED
ENTRANCE TO TWO
FLATS

AFTER STYLISH
HALL TO A FAMILY
HOME

Partitioned off at some point in its life, this hallway (above) was reinstated to its original form and treated to a delightful mural (above right). On a practical note: a fitted length of matting at the door is more useful than a small mat.

A hall is the first impression visitors have of the home—some never get beyond it—so it is worth giving its decoration the same careful consideration shown to other rooms. This painted hall demonstrates how much can be achieved in what is usually a neglected area.

When the stud partition of the hall (above) was removed, it was discovered that the banisters, newel post and handrail had all been sawn away. Reproductions were dutifully made and installed and the damaged floor covered with a new strip beech floor, sealed so that it only needs cleaning with a mop.

The magnificent mural is an allusion to the world of architecture in which the owners are involved, and the painter was asked to give the work a strong architectural bias. After considering various ideas the final choice was a mural based on Le Corbusier's Villa Savoie. The shapes are derived from his plans and elevations for the building and the mural has been painted in delicate shades of eggshell paint, the design reflected in fascinating ways by the panelled mirror/coat stand. The classical still-life of lilies and fluted plaster column add a perfect finish to a serene and uncluttered entrance.

Dado ducks

The humbler cottage staircase and landing (right) also has a mural, but it is in complete contrast to the graphic approach of the previous hall. This one is a trompe l'oeil, full of clouds and open windows with a joky seagull light

completing the outdoor theme. A painting job like this is really for the professionals, but the staircase (above) with its decorative dado frieze of Egyptian-style ducks is something which could be tackled by an enthusiastic amateur. A repeat pattern makes life much easier and there is no reason why the ducks couldn't be cut from stencils although these have been drawn free-hand. (For help on stencils, see page 148.) By way of a change, the staircase steps are only painted on the risers with the treads stained to match the floorboards. Another idea which looks impressive on a carpetless stairway is to leave the tread natural, but to paint and stencil a pattern on the risers. This is guaranteed to give an impressive effect as you look up the stairs from the front door.

The great outdoors and the world of ancient Egypt (above and left) give these hallways strong identities. Too many halls are usually remarkable only for their anonymity.

MASTERING DISGUISES

Disguises can involve all sorts of crafty ploys for masking inherent faults around the house. Unsightly runs of central heating pipes, for instance, or ugly views from a window, bad plasterwork and so on can all be masked by clever subterfuge. There are two methods of approach you can choose from, either the 'play-it-down' or the 'cover-it-up' variety. Both are illustrated here.

This bathroom (left) had a dingy view out onto the wall of a block of flats. It provided little light so was covered up entirely and a handsome mirror hung in front. Recessed downlighters in the ceiling now provide the light source.

Items will recede if they are painted the same colour as the wall. This undistinguished headboard (above) 'disappears' by being spray-painted to match its surroundings. Maybe carried away by success, the sprayer ran amok, giving both the table and telephone a similar spattered look.

A roughly painted trellis covering this ceiling (right) might have looked rather stark but is enhanced by being strung with baskets of dried flowers. This sort of device is especially useful for small rooms which have ceilings proportionally too high for their size. Fabric could also be used.

Damaged plasterwork can be covered over simply by panelling. Here (left) painted tongue and groove boards add an air of the Twenties and Thirties to this bathroom. Taps of that period and an old basin which once graced the Savoy Hotel add to the atmosphere. Less damaged plaster above the dado is covered with a thick, marble-look wallpaper.

Behind the fake tiled door above (the tiles are actually wallpaper) beats the heart of a washing machine, never the most lovely of items and much better hidden out of the way in a convenient alcove than catching attention in the kitchen.

BATHROOMS

DOUBLE EXPOSURE

BEFORE DATED, SEVENTIES-LOOK BATHROOM

AFTER STREAM-LINED EIGHTIES BATHROOM

A bathroom badly in need of updating (above) has been given a completely new look without the expense of changing any of the basic fittings.

It is hard to recognize the new bathroom from the old here, although neither the appliances nor the tiles have been altered; the change may be dramatic but is purely decorative. In a space as small as 3.75 sq m (40 sq ft) the cardinal rule is to keep it simple: colours have therefore been restricted to yellow and white and overpowering patterns are taboo. Mirrors are used to the maximum, with two large ones set opposite each other so that light reflections and space seem to go on to infinity.

Yellow metal shelving stands over the lavatory, where space would otherwise have been wasted, and although the shelves' narrow depth barely stands proud of the cistern, there is plenty of space to store numerous towels, hair-dryer, and so on.

The shower area has been completely screened off with an arrangement resembling a modern tent: the material is lightweight and waterproof (like yacht sails) with a cut-out oval 'door' which is fitted with a waterproof plastic zip. It is held in place by a length of dowel slotted through a hem at the top and another at the bottom which is slightly weighted to keep it taught. Also along the bottom of the fabric is a 10 cm (4 in) wide strip of material; this hangs over the shower tray so that water cannot dribble out onto the floor.

A matching yellow and white floor, yellow taps and towel rails complete this simple but effective scheme lit by two sentinel strip lights.

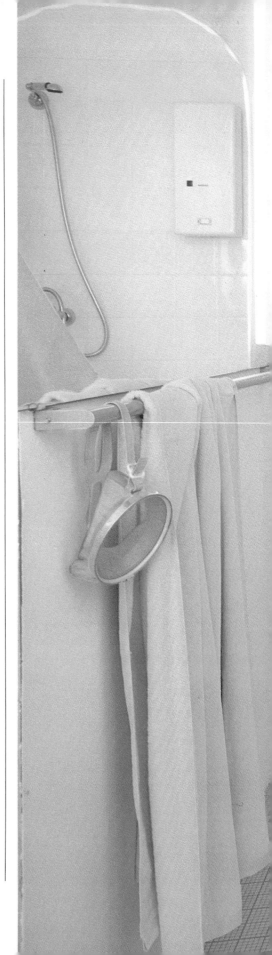

MAKING SPACE

BEFORE CUPBOARD IN A CORRIDOR

AFTER CORRIDOR BATHROOM WHICH DOUBLES IN SIZE

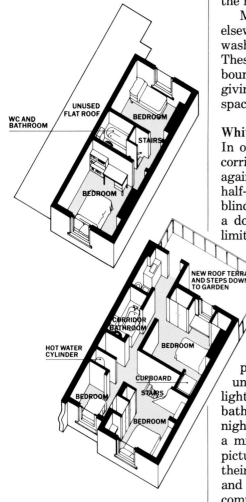

The key to the clever adaptability of this bathroom is the doors which can be used in various different permutations, depending on the needs of the moment. There are three possibilities: with the doors closed *parallel* to the corridor, the bathroom is a narrow cloakroom style area; with the doors closed *across* the corridor, the bathroom doubles its size and is a spacious bathing area; and, thirdly, with the door to the bedroom left *open* and the other bathroom door closed *across* the corridor, it becomes an en suite bathroom. The diagram (left) should make this design wizardry clearer.

Although it was not possible to have a conventional window, the bathroom is kept light and airy despite its corridor positioning by a skylight which has mirrored sides to reflect extra light into the room.

Mirror is also used with great effect elsewhere: alongside the bath, above the washbasin and along the corridor wall. These all reflect into each other and bounce the light about, at the same time giving the visual effect of doubling up the space.

White for light

In order not to lose the view along the corridor onto a flower-filled terrace and, again, to let in more light the doors are half-glazed and have plain white roller blinds for privacy. One door is fitted with a double towel rail since space was so limited that it couldn't be squeezed in elsewhere.

To link the bathroom with the corridor and to maintain a harmonious entity to the scheme, both are decorated in the same simple, but effective, way. Walls and ceiling are white-painted tongue and groove wooden panelling—always a good disguise for uneven walls (see page 101). Down-lighters and a recessed strip light above the bath-side mirror illuminate the area at night. Used against this plain background, a mixed selection of potted plants and pictures are thrown into prominence, their presence supplying the finishing and softening touches required to complete the bathroom's effect.

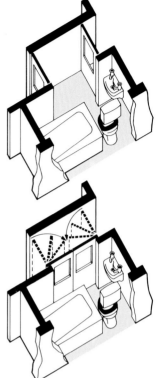

The first floor of the house was largely remodelled (far left) and increased in size by building onto a single-storey extension. Inside, clever combinations of the same two doors can alter the bathroom (left) from a small corridor room to a larger version or even to an en suite arrangement. The plans (above) show two of the three possibilities.

EDWARDIAN ELEGANCE

BEFORE BADLY PLANNED, MEDIOCRE BATHROOM

AFTER EDWARDIAN-STYLE CLOAKROOM-CUM-BATHROOM

An old, prettily flowered lavatory, rescued from a site, was the starting off point for this period bathroom. It set the tone for an atmosphere reminiscent of an Edwardian cloakroom which the owners were keen to create for this, their second bathroom of the house—used mainly by visiting friends. The authentic old bath, wash-hand basin and taps were picked up by scouring junk and antique shops, although facsimiles are now being produced by various manufacturers.

Once the basics were assembled, professional help was employed to plan the room and to design the panelling which surrounds the fittings; the wood may look like deeply burnished mahogany but in fact it is softwood deceptively painted to look more expensive and then varnished to resist steam and water splashes. The mirror, which is another junk shop find, was given the same treatment, as was the flat lid to the lavatory which conceals it in true thunderbox fashion.

The modern, metal-framed window was far from being in keeping with the old-fashioned theme of the room and was brought into line by being framed with moulding painted to match the rest of the wood. A plain holland blind is kept at half mast during the day to hide metal glazing bars.

Walls and ceiling may look like marble but the pattern is merely painted in warm yellow pink tones; however the floor is the real thing. Worn with age and once laid in an old dairy, it has now been varnished to protect it from staining and to give it extra depth of colour. At one end of the bath is a period glass-fronted cabinet used to display various toiletries—antique or junk shops often yield interesting alternatives to the modern medicine cabinet.

Other furnishings were chosen equally carefully: the heating is supplied by a veritable old giant of a radiator and the lighting is also suitably Edwardian (but powered by electricity, not gas...).

To complete the cloakroom atmosphere, a selection of appropriate pictures in traditional frames crowd the walls.

A switch of bathroom suite and period (above and right). This reproduction of an Edwardian cloakroom employs much fakery of marble and mahogany.

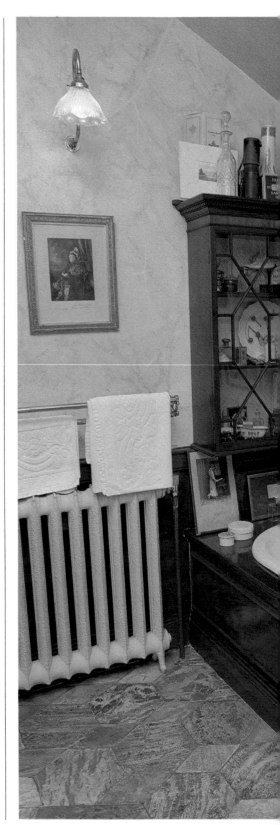

Appropriate pictures in traditional frames crowd the walls to complete the comfortable cloak-room atmosphere (above), while an old original decorated lavatory bowl is hidden in an old original way.

FOLD-AWAY SANUA

The bathroom was neatly designed to fit under the slope of a flight of stairs. This has been repositioned during renovation, as had the overall layout of the house (right).

BEFORE
PASSAGE AND GENERAL STAIRCASE AREA

AFTER
COMBINED BATHROOM AND SAUNA

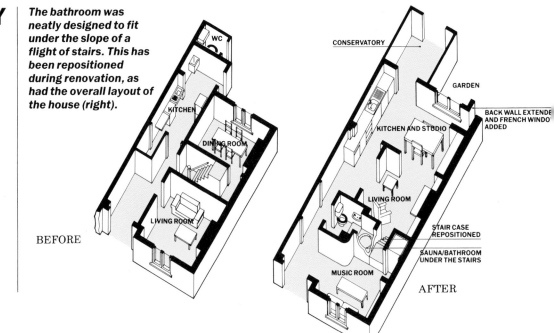

BEFORE

WC

KITCHEN

DINING ROOM

LIVING ROOM

CONSERVATORY

GARDEN

BACK WALL EXTENDED AND FRENCH WINDOW ADDED

KITCHEN AND STUDIO

LIVING ROOM

STAIR CASE REPOSITIONED

SAUNA/BATHROOM UNDER THE STAIRS

MUSIC ROOM

AFTER

A second bathroom and a cloakroom for guests were all that the owners initially had in mind, but it wasn't long before they realized that it would be not much more complicated and also rather nice to have a sauna as well, and so their dual-purpose bathroom was born. The design is as concise as that found in the cabin of a boat, where no space is wasted, since the main area of the room measures only 1.7 m×2 m (5.7×6.5 ft). The small round bath and shower area are additional, neatly fitted under the slope of the stairs.

Transformation from washing room to sauna simply involves unhinging the bench with mirror fixed to its underside, laying it down over the lavatory and washbasin, shutting the doors to the bath and turning up the temperature.

There are a couple of other small benches to sit on and the bath is reached by one narrow door for that final, numbingly cold plunge or shower. The sauna stove stands in a corner protected by rails and excess water which is thrown onto it, or just splashed and dripped by bathers, runs away through a drain in the tiled floor.

Installing a sauna requires all sorts of specialist knowledge on insulation, etc., and consequently this one was fitted by an expert firm. There should be no condensation problems as a sauna provides dry heat. In this house, the minimal amount of heat that does escape goes directly up the stairwell to the upstairs landing; and as the sauna is mainly used in winter it can be a useful back-up to the central heating!

The bathroom as a sauna (above left) and the bathroom as its nature intended (above). The change of use involves merely hinging down a bench over the miniature washbasin and lavatory and shutting the door to the bath.

JAPANESE SIMPLICITY

BEFORE DULL,
WINDOWLESS ROOM

AFTER JAPANESE-
STYLE BATHING
ROOM WITH
FILTERED
DAYLIGHT

*A basic, small upstairs
room with a sloping
ceiling (above) is turned
into a plausible
Japanese bathing area
with the addition of a
few key references,
such as a shoji screen
and rosewood floor.
The fireplace and
chimney breast were
renovated when the
adjacent wall was
knocked out.*

A love of the simplicity and beauty of the traditional Japanese style of living prompted the owner of this bathroom to recreate its atmospheric calm.

The room was first stripped of all clutter, including a wall of fitted cupboards; one wall was knocked out and substituted with a traditional, tailor-made wood and paper shoji screen which allowed daylight from the adjacent dressing room to filter softly through to the bathroom. These screens usually slide but in this location it was not feasible, so the conventional door was concealed by covering it with sheet mirror.

The walls demonstrate what clever subterfuge can be effected with paint. They were created by masters in the field of fakery—film screen painters—and their gently faded and aged-plaster appearance was skilfully copied from a photograph of the walls in the old palace of Katsura. The lovely wooden flooring is of rosewood strips, treated with oil for six months rather than varnished and now regularly polished to perfection; polished floors develop an attractive patina with age which those sealed with varnish can never achieve, but it takes a special dedication to bear the extra work of all that waxing.

Copper finish

The magnificent deep copper bath was a lucky find in France, although a free-standing Victorian tub suitably painted on the outside would make an effective alternative. It stands on an austere plinth of matt oatmeal tiles and was originally re-coppered; afterwards it was toned-down and aged by three days of hard rubbing with wire wool because it looked too new. The perfect taps to complement such an unusual tub proved impossible to find, so the neat solution was to recess the tap heads out of sight behind the bath, leaving just the water spout visible. The floor-resting basin posed the same matching-up problem and functional laboratory taps provided the answer for this second fake: the basin may look like hollowed-out stone but in actual fact it is pottery.

Abundant plain white towels are

warmed by a snaking copper towel rail that was made to order by a plumber from central heating piping and attached to the wall with industrial clips. This also helps heat the room, as do the central heating pipes laid under the floor, unintentionally but conveniently keeping the rosewood warm.

Candles, the owner felt, would have

been the perfect lighting for such a room, but practicality prevailed and recessed ceiling lights and a small lamp (operated outside the room for safety) were installed instead for a similar soft effect. Another change was necessary for practical reasons: the traditional floor-level basin has now been replaced by a more accessible waist-high antique washstand. But the bathroom has lost none of its tranquil atmosphere and is still kept as simple and soothingly empty as possible. No toiletries are on show—they are kept in a small recessed cupboard with a rosewood door—while such an intrusive modern device as an extractor fan is elegantly camouflaged with a rosewood grill.

COUNTRY COMFORT

BEFORE MUCH NEGLECTED COTTAGE BATHROOM

AFTER COUNTRY-STYLE BATHROOM, INEXPENSIVELY ACHIEVED

A towering water tank gave this bathroom a prison camp air (above) which the owner quickly altered into an ultra-feminine country atmosphere (right).

'A ghastly mess' was how the owner of this bathroom described it when she first saw it. There was a cold water tank towering beside the basin and the decoration, such as it was, had not been touched for years. Uppermost in her mind was what *not* to do with the bathroom. Being very anxious to avoid giving her cottage a townie-down-for-the-weekend look and an over-decorated air, the aim was simple country style. There was also a tight budget to consider, so fancy fittings were avoided in favour of the plainest possible of bathroom suites and taps—much to the horror of her plumber.

The bulky water tank was the first to go and the new basin moved into the space it left. The owner would have preferred to leave the basin under the window, but then there would have been nowhere to put the mirrors. Replacing the glass panes in the window with mirror glass would have been a neat solution to the problem but in this instance would have spoilt the view and cut out too much light.

Fashioning frames
Despairing of ever finding the right size of old cupboard or chest in which to insert the washbasin, she gave up foot-slogging around the shops and decided it would be simpler to have something made to measure. She designed the shape of a curving frame to put around the basin and a matching one for the bath and had them made from new pine. To age the appearance of the wood she used a darkening stain, then rubbed it back and finished with matt ('*never* shiny') varnish. Cupboard doors under the basin were kept simple and painted to match the boxed-in bath, which has doors at each end to keep unsightly bathroom paraphernalia at hand but conveniently out of sight.

The final touch was originally going to be draping the bath recess with fabric, rather in the manner of a French campaign bed, but this never happened and anyway may have looked too ostentatious for country living. Instead an extravagantly ruched blind was fitted and the walls painted a bluey grey

matched to a toning carpet. Accessories such as a wall-cupboard and towel rail are kept to the pine theme and an armchair (not in the picture) gives the room an extra touch of comfort.

VARIATIONS

An armchair (or some other similar sort of comfortable seating) is one of the touchstones for creating the restful atmosphere of a country bathroom, along

with other traditional pieces of furniture, pictures and so on. Strictly speaking, these furnishings are more conducive to instant atmosphere if they are old and consequently a bit battered, but modern adaptations of simple, country-style furniture are readily available and would happily substitute.

Natural textures are important too, such as wood and rush, cane and cotton and country tiles. No plastic or brash

113

Three varying ways (right and far right) of creating a country-style bathroom. They share in common a simplicity of touch and natural materials—with not a plastic nailbrush in sight.

colours, nothing shiny and new must intrude. A true country bathroom should be a little worn around the edges. The one (above right) follows all the right rules, with a loose cover over an old chair, draped fabric and a shawl over an old table and (out of the picture) gathered fabric around a washstand—a cheaper and simpler solution than fitted wooden doors. The whole scheme is drawn together by its muted pinks; pictures, rugs, cushions and personal knick-knacks make it seem more like a small sitting room than a wash place.

The tiled bathroom (above), which is in the same house, was constructed from two smaller rooms and it too achieves in a more restrained way a French country feel. Traditional tiles were finished off at head-height with a moulding which successfully gives an expensive look; cheap calico blinds hide modern windows but still let in light. An old mirror has been painted blue to match the tiles and

114

hangs above the marble washstand, which like the bath (not shown) is fairly simply panelled and fitted with a length of skirting board along the bottom—another effective decorator's trick for giving an expensive look.

An old chair, cane basket, pretty china and cotton rug plus period lighting are the perfect accessories; and, essential to any country bathroom, there are always flowers. Fresh or dried they are the all-important finishing touch.

ALL IN ONE

BEFORE
BATHROOM IN AN
OLD, FLAT-ROOFED
BRICK EXTENSION

AFTER
BATHROOM IN A
NEW, STEEL
EXTENSION

A falling ninety-foot tree caused the sudden demise of the old bathroom and extension at the back of this 18th-century house and the owner, an architect, designed the replacement structure himself.

He used a coated-steel cladding system normally intended for industrial buildings; only two inches (5 cm) thick, it has high thermal rating, but he also chose it because it was lightweight, clean, quick to erect and, in building terms, dry. This was of particular advantage since sole access to the building site was through the house and it would avoid having workmen bundling bricks and messy mortar and water through his home.

To complement his newly-designed extension, the architect chose an equally arresting bathroom interior, one that was literally centred on a sculptured glass-fibre construction of whirlpool bath and two handbasins. Sited in the middle of the room, it allows family traffic to flow freely. The floor has been specially stepped so that the children can climb easily into the bath, and the lavatory and bidet are hidden out of sight behind it. The carpeted shelf conceals all the plumbing. This moulded unit was obviously specially manufactured, but it would be possible to copy the free-standing island unit idea with a combination of more conventional bathroom fittings and some custom-made woodwork.

Leading from the foreground of the picture is the entrance to the bathroom,

The old back extension before its sudden demise (far left). The new steel-clad design (centre) houses a terrace as well as a de luxe bathroom. Inside, the bathroom suite has an unusual central position, with the lavatory and bidet out of sight in a stepped-down area beyond the bath.

made up of white perspex and wood sliding screens which allow light from the bathroom to pass through to the adjoining mosaic-tiled shower room and linen cupboard area. The light travels through to a landing on the stairs and from this vantage point there is a tunnelled vista back out across the bath into the treetops.

Pale pink and blue are the unexpectedly gentle colours chosen to decorate this rather hard-edged room and the subsequent addition (since the picture was taken) of pale blue see-through curtains adds to the softening effect. The column is concrete, wrapped with pale blue vinyl floorcovering. And note the unusual soap dishes—they are pencil boxes.

COLOURFUL AND QUIRKY

BEFORE EMPTY LOFT SPACE

AFTER INEXPENSIVE AND IDIOSYNCRATIC BATHROOM

A patchwork quilt of tiles (above right) echoes the deliberately-mismatched bathroom suite. This bathroom has been sited next to another (as shown in the plan) and they handily share a communal cupboard, built into the dividing wall. The kitchen shown on the plan is the one featured on pages 16–17.

The origins of this bathroom design were dictated by a bargain too good to refuse from a local shop selling off a motley selection of redundant stock remarkably cheaply—separate items of bathroom suite, each in a different colour. Such was the attraction that the owner went ahead and installed her own, highly individual, multi-pastel-coloured bathroom suite. After all, who's to say that a washbasin *must* match its pedestal?

Thereafter it was simply a question of playing up the multi-coloured theme. The owner, appropriately enough a well-

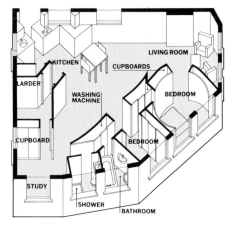

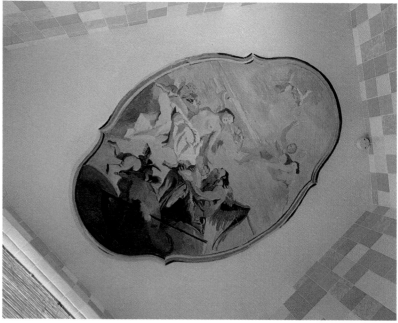

Something other than the taps to gaze at whilst having a bath (above). This romantically-painted ceiling is literally the bathroom's crowning glory.

between floor and wall, along the window ledge and around the mirror.

A cheap bamboo blind and some even cheaper garden trellis provide privacy at the window and once the greenery has grown along the window sill it will provide a more effective visual barrier.

To lie back in the bath and gaze heavenwards brings the biggest surprise because there, on the ceiling, is a replica of the kind of painting usually associated with finer, older buildings. A love of renaissance and baroque ceilings inspired the owner to ask a painter friend to complete his first fake. She loves the quirkiness of having such an unlikely grandiose statement in such an inappropriate setting. It makes something special of the room (but something simpler is advisable for untrained amateurs pursuing Sistine Chapel leanings.)

Next door to this bathroom is another, smaller one with a shower intended for guests and/or children. It, too, has the same colour theme, but here the tiles are arranged in horizontal bands—one black and two multi-coloured. The bathrooms also share the same cupboard: a hole has been knocked through the dividing wall and each bathroom has its own set of mirrored-tile doors leading into it.

known ceramist, bought up plenty of inexpensive standard tiles in matching pastels and proceeded to use them in an effective patchwork pattern right up to the ceiling. Just using the pastels alone would have been too much of a good thing and as a relief and something of a dramatic contrast, a black band of tiles was inserted to act as a break. Below this the pastels are arranged in diagonal stripes before the black once again appears on the floor in the form of black quarry tiles. Quarter round edging tiles are used to finish off neatly the joins

SKY-HIGH VIEW

BEFORE EMPTY LOFT SPACE

AFTER BATHROOM WITH SUNKEN TUB AND SEPARATE DRESSING AREA

Rather than lower the window (above) so that the view could be seen, the bath was raised instead (right).

It would have been sacrilege not to make use of the magnificent view from this loft so the designer decided to raise the floor level of one section of the bathroom up to the bottom of the window so that bathers could lounge in the tub and gaze out onto the Hudson River. The made-to-measure bath is luxuriously large and lined with the same matt grey, non-slip tiles as those covering the steps, floor and walls. The tub has angled inner sides, as do the steps which lead up to it in such an appropriately grand manner. Something similar could be copied in more modest surroundings by raising the floor level in one or two stages alongside a conventional bath; it is an old decorator's trick for adding a sumptuous touch to a room and always looks effective.

Real candlelight is also guaranteed to add something special to the atmosphere, so a candelabra was chosen and fitted out accordingly, being backed up by more conventional downlighters as needed. The remaining half of the bathroom is the dressing area and to emphasize it as separate it has been decorated differently, in white with a wooden floor. The wall which divides the two areas has been given simple, sculptural cut-outs to allow light through and also to provide enticing views of the Hudson river beyond. The lavatory is hidden away between this wall and that of the sunken bath. A long simple white laminate shelf holds the washbasin and above it is a large semi-circular mirror positioned to reflect the window opposite. Plenty of built-in closet space is available between the window and the double door: two narrow doors with etched glass panels make a fitting combination to give an appropriately theatrical entrance to this quietly dramatic bathroom.

The dressing area is divided from the bathing section, although it is still possible to see the view through the cut-out openings (above). The bathroom is saved from looking austere by pots of lush palms (left).

SHIP SHAPE

BEFORE TINY,
SPARSE AND BADLY
PLANNED

AFTER COMPACT
AND IMAGINATIVE

The position of the sink in this bare room (above) was moved away from the window to create more space. The redesign (right) is kept simple and unfussy, necessary in a small space.

Measuring only 1.5 m (5 ft) square, the confines of this bathroom were very limiting, but the architect owner has achieved a stunning effect with the in-built galley compactness of a boat. To reinforce this feeling there are nautical touches such as a sliding door into the bathroom, which sports a real porthole.

As elsewhere in the apartment, green studded rubber flooring covers the badly pitted walls and the various built-in chipboard fittings. The bathroom suite has been replaced and moved and the space visually simplified where possible; for instance, boxing in the cistern makes the redesign more streamlined.

There is a place for everything—even the bathroom scales have a special hang-up—and there are two built-in cupboards, one fronted by a black metal door, the other above the washbasin with a plastic roller shutter. Industrial components such as these are used with imagination throughout the flat: sucker holders for carrying large panes of glass double as door handles; perforated metal is made into furniture, and yachting equipment (again, the nautical theme) is used for cushions, and so on (see page 60). It is always worth looking at the equipment provided by specialist suppliers for it can often provide individual and practical solutions to home design problems.

Light and bright
The swivelling mirror beside the built-in basin has fluorescent tube lighting running down beside it for honest face-to-face appraisal, while back views are reflected in a large mirror covering the opposite wall above the bath. Both mirrors help visually to increase the size of the room. On the third side of the bath is a plastic-coated grid for additional storage of articles such as towels, and on the floor are black plastic open grid tiles. Jolly yellow accessories and pink towels are the final touch to 'lift' the black of the floor and the strong green of the walls.

To enforce the simplicity of the room, Venetian blinds have been used to cover the windows. However, it is the use of colour which provides the impact to transform this small and once undistinguished bathroom.

GLASS HOUSE

BEFORE PART OF AN EMPTY LOFT SPACE

AFTER AN ELEGANT DOUBLE BATHROOM

The designers of this bathroom were determined to make it a gracious room despite the fact that all the walls would have to be interior and windowless. To make it feel like a 'real' room, not just a boxed space, they introduced changes of level in the floor and ceiling which help break up the square shape and give added visual interest—the horizontal bands of dark tiles not only draw attention to these changes, they also help deceive the eye into thinking the room larger than it really is.

To anyone unimpressed by the lack of style of ready-made shower cabinets, the curving walls of the glass brick shower area will demonstrate a spectacular alternative. Almost sculptural in its design, the circular shape is a perfect counterfoil to the predominately hard-edged room and its naturally enclosing form means that no shower door is needed. The electric ceiling light inside the shower diffuses through the glass into the bathroom and cleverly gives the impression of filtered daylight compensating for the fact that there are no windows.

The recessed tub is a double one and there are also two washbasins, practically a necessity in a busy household if you have only one bathroom and no bedroom basins. The glass brick theme is continued here with a dividing wall between wash hand basins and lavatory.

The layout of the bathroom (right) allows for two washbasins and a double tub (far right). The room is meticulously tiled throughout with glass bricks forming a rounded, sculptural shower area, a stylish alternative to the more usual shower cabinet.

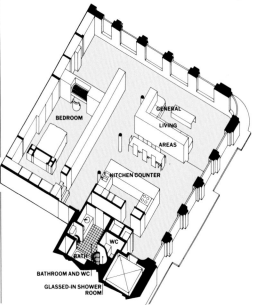

BEDROOM

GENERAL LIVING AREAS

KITCHEN COUNTER

WC

BATH

BATHROOM AND WC

GLASSED-IN SHOWER ROOM

A large mirror, outlined with lightbulbs in true theatrical dressing room style, gives excellent and—be warned—honest light. For one-hundred-per-cent-groomers an all-important back-of-the-head view is provided by a built-in storage cupboard with mirrored front on the opposite wall. Smaller toiletry and medicinal items are kept behind shallow, sliding mirror doors directly above the washbasins and under a shelf.

Ceramic tiles are matt throughout to avoid the overwhelming shiny effect of glazed tiles in such a small area. Any tiled area must be executed meticulously and here, with the same tiles on floor and ceiling, the grouting lines match perfectly. Finally, accessories are white in order not to detract from the simple, elegance of the overall design.

If you have enough space, double basins ease bathroom congestion in a busy household (above). Here, small bathroom necessities are stored under the shelf and behind sliding mirrored doors.

CREATIVE TILING

Rather than buying one design of tile and considering the creative part of the decorating job done, think again. Combinations of tiles can create unusual and original effects: old with new, patterned with plain, plains used together to form borders and designs, and so on. They will ensure that a kitchen or bathroom is given a unique and therefore more interesting treatment.

One way of clearing the china cabinet also gives an appealing theme to the bathroom (above). The plates which crowd the walls could have been bought to match the tiles, or the other way round. A similar crisp idea could be copied in other colours for the kitchen or a separate lavatory.

A combination of new, plain tiles and old, patterned ones has been used imaginatively to form this over-sized and original fireplace (left).

A checkerboard bathroom created with inexpensive tiles (above). The pattern is saved from being too overwhelming by the use of strong, bright hues which both counteract it and act as a colourful relief.

Besides covering the walls, mosaic tiles form both bath and basin (left). The utter simplicity of the design uses a diamond motif for decoration: along the cornice, as cupboard door 'handles', and as a cut-out to let light through to the shower.

An unlikely combination of three different designs of tiles (above and left), but one which works well. The idea of outlining the different heights of the tables and cooker is practical as well as effective and much more visually interesting than a straight border would have been.

BEDROOMS

CLASSICAL DREAM

BEFORE ROOM OVERWHELMED BY FITTED UNITS

AFTER FANTASY BEDROOM

Stark bold fronts of boring fitted cupboards in the original bedroom (right) have now been eclipsed by a decorative fantasy (far right). Furnishings are kept to a simply-shaped minimum so as not to compete with the ethereal theme.

Rather than rip out the fitted cupboards which were inherited from the previous occupants and hated, the new owners thought of an alternative plan to thwart their ugliness. They attacked with pots of paint. The cupboards, which take up space along three walls of the bedroom, were transformed with coats of bright white paint from the original sickly blue and dirty white, while fussy brass handles were changed to plain white ones. With this new, clean-lined look the cupboards were then ready literally to pale into insignificance compared to the fantasy which was planned for the rest of the room.

The owners wanted clouds all over the walls and ceiling—the real thing and not cartoon style, cotton wool ones. The ethereal and realistic effect that is the end result was achieved with an air-brushing technique. Carpeting, especially the shag pile sort they inherited with the cupboards, would have been wrong to complement such visual lightness, so they plumped for marble. Or at least what looks like marble. In fact the flooring is laminate which has been cut into two foot (0.6 m) squares, attached to half inch plywood, then laid to break up the original laminate patterning. Although it has been down for some time, this surface has worn well but would not be appropriate for heavy duty areas. The same marble laminate was also used to cover the fitted cupboard surfaces.

The columns are refugees from a film set and were at first thought too short so that it was originally planned to make heightening plinths for them to reach the ceiling. However their lack of stature turned out to be an advantage: because they end a foot or so short they somehow create a more realistic effect and make the room seem higher than it really is.

For the final touches to this neo-classical scene, jokey golden cherubs float about in the 'sky' and a Roman bust surveys the scene, but the furniture, the bulkhead lights and the Venetian blinds are all hard-edged modern accessories which combine with the theme surprisingly well.

ROMANTIC DIVISIONS

BEFORE LARGE STUDY/BEDROOM

AFTER BEDROOM WITH HALLWAY, STORAGE, SLEEPING AND SITTING AREAS

This large bedroom is subdivided into areas for storage, sleeping and so on by yards of gathered fabric which form the delineating 'walls' (below and right). Combined with old shawls, flowers and patchwork, the effect is dramatically romantic.

The occupant of this bedroom did not intentionally set out to create such a romantic mood. His previous bedroom was more akin to a theatre dressing room with clothes arrayed on wheeled dress rails or, when space ran out on those, hung from the picture rail. Faced with a large, featureless open space 24 ft (7.5 m) square he decided to divide it up into sections and was on the point of getting in a carpenter when it was cleverly suggested that fabric should be used instead of solid partitions for the subdivisions.

He wanted the bedroom to fulfil four different functions: for storing clothes, for sleeping in, for sitting in, and as an entrance hall. The hall, he felt, was important to create an air of mystery and add an element of surprise; it should ensure that anyone walking in would not immediately realize the true size of the room. This is the kind of philosophy he employed when designing gardens, the creation of unexpected unseen areas making for a more interesting and exciting design.

Once the positioning of the sections was worked out (see plan), 330 ft (100 m) of fabric (double the combined length of the new 'walls') were needed and were luckily bought cheaply in the form of glazed cotton in a sale. Glazed cotton is excellent for keeping off dust—the curtain frills are unglazed and quickly lost their pristine crispness by comparison. Battens were then attached to the floor and to the ceiling, the fabric hemmed and slotted through (see page

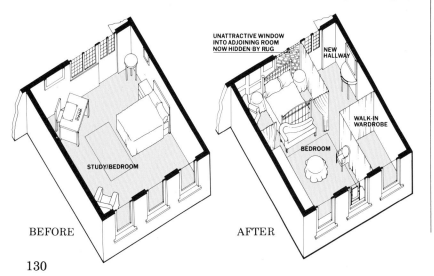

STUDY/BEDROOM

UNATTRACTIVE WINDOW INTO ADJOINING ROOM NOW HIDDEN BY RUG

NEW HALLWAY

WALK-IN WARDROBE

BEDROOM

BEFORE

AFTER

157); taking it down again for cleaning is equally simple. Once the gathered fabric walls were up, the designer decided to go for a totally romantic look and began to add the appropriate frills, flowers and lace.

The window into the adjacent dining room was concealed with a Thirties American patchwork quilt, and an unsightly modern fireplace hidden behind a giant double wardrobe which, because it is painted white like the walls, does not overwhelm the room as might otherwise have been the case. Other storage space is found behind the fabric walls in one corner.

In contrast to the picture-crammed walls around the bed, the windows are left uncluttered, partly because the bedroom is not overlooked, but also because the owner finds curtains visually heavy. Instead he has draped a beautiful piece of lace at one window, leaving the others bare. The focal point of this sitting area is the quilt-draped table and its generously filled basket of dried flowers, around which the chaise longue and other seating is grouped.

The entrance area is far more formally and symmetrically furnished, its severity the perfect foil for the soft, pretty room beyond. With so much going on in this and the other areas the choice of colours and flooring was kept as simple as possible. The walls are white, with blue around the brass bed to define it as a separate area. The flooring is practical coir matting, which also provides a contrast in texture, enlivened here and there with soft rugs.

The restrained entrance to the bedroom (left) acts as a foil to the overtly romantic scene beyond. A picture hanging in front of the gathered fabric 'wall' makes it appear more solid. The magnificent white-painted wardrobe (above) is the same colour as the walls, merging with, rather than dominating, the scene.

PLATFORM ONE

BEFORE PART OF AN OLD SCHOOL HALL

AFTER UPPER LEVEL BEDROOM WITH DRESSING, BATH AND UTILITY ROOMS UNDERNEATH

The corner of a redundant school hall (above) provided plenty of height in which to build a raised bedroom (right) uncluttered by clothes storage; this is hidden below stairs.

The owners here were keen to create an unencumbered bedroom, one which was devoid of clothes storage or washing. Calm and clutter free, it would have a bed, books and maybe a table and chairs. As well as having plenty of floor space in their home—it is a large, old school hall—they also had plenty of height, so their architect advised them to build upwards. This way a sleeping area could be created upstairs with a walk-in dressing room, bathroom and utility room concealed underneath. Since the couple didn't require a large bathroom, just somewhere functional and easy to use, this plan worked perfectly and fitted into a the available space (see plan).

For those with a more conventional home it is still possible to have a similar sort of arrangement without building a platform. Use instead a spare bedroom as a combined dressing room/utility room or even bathroom; a small lavatory could be concealed in a run of fitted cupboards. It makes sense and is a rare treat to leave a bedroom free of clothes storage and to have a separate room to cater entirely for washing (be it yourself or your clothes).

It was the architect who also suggested the Japanese-influenced platform structure in this room. The white-painted partition walls are plasterboard, decorated with wooden beading, and the door into the dressing room is treated in the same manner so that it is invisible when shut. The grid pattern of the safety rail is echoed in the arrangement of the storage square under the stairs (which is to be fitted with a handrail to comply with building regulations), and despite the valuable storage area they provide, the open rectangles would also look pleasingly sculptural if left virtually empty.

Up on the platform, the brick arch is emphasized by shelves which have been cut to size to follow its curve, while who-ever sits at the table is treated to a panoramic view of the sitting/dining/kitchen area which can be seen through the folding half-glazed partition that separates this from the bedroom.

LAUNDRY

BATHROOM/WC

WALK-IN WARDROBE

STEPS TO SLEEPING AREA

Beneath the sleeping platform, and neatly tucked away out of sight, is a walk-in wardrobe. Conveniently sited next to the laundry, it is in turn conveniently sited next to the bathroom—so body and shirts can be cleaned at the same time.

MADE TO MEASURE

BEFORE SMALL ROOMS WITH LIMITED SPACE FOR BEDS

AFTER SPACE-SAVING SLEEPING PLATFORMS

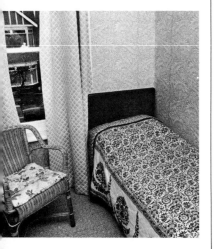

The conventional sort of arrangement usually to be found in small bedrooms is shown above. The two bedrooms (right and far right) demonstrate how things can be turned around to their own advantage.

The two sleeping arrangements shown here demonstrate a similar way of coping with a tight spot. In both cases the beds stretch from wall to wall but, being contained, are far less obtrusive than those in conventional bedrooms.

A children's room in pink and blue (right) utilizes an alcove for a bunk arrangement, leaving the rest of the room free for a play area, desks and storage. The bunk sleeping platforms are made from wood and fitted with metal grilles to keep their small occupants safe inside. Steps to the top bunk are formed into a squared 'spiral' staircase, and also double as storage space. The simple pink and blue theme, carried through to carpet and

accessories, makes a welcome change from the often-used primary colours in children's rooms.

The platform bed (above) saves on space with its unusual placing across the room and directly under a window. Most people would automatically have left the window free, ignoring this area's possibilities. Space under the bed is also exploited to house a plan chest and cupboards. Walls and woodwork are all painted the same restful blue. Keeping to one colour—including even the bed-linen—increases a feeling of space. A shelf full of plants at the window provides a more stylish alternative to the ubiquitous net curtain.

ALL-PURPOSE SCAFFOLD

BEFORE TOP OF
THE HOUSE BOXROOM

AFTER COMBINED
BEDROOM AND
STUDY

An undistinguished small boxroom (above) was given a new lease of life by removing the chimney breast and the ceiling. Into this newly-created space were packed a wardrobe, bed, desk and shelving—a feat that probably only a scaffolding system (right) could achieve.

The owners, designers, looked upwards for the extra space needed to turn a small room at the top of the house into somewhere comfortable enough both to sleep and work. The solution was to knock out the ceiling and expose the rafters of the pitched roof, and to avoid heat loss these were then insulated and plaster-boarded over. To let in extra light an electrically operated window was installed which also gives necessary ventilation—it can get rather hot and stuffy sleeping near the roof. For the same reason, the window has a special blind with an aluminium backing which reflects the sun's rays and avoids any heat build up. It is also useful for keeping out the sunlight very efficiently, which prevents too many early-morning awakenings. To make even more space the chimney breast was also removed.

Flexible fittings

Into this newly-created area was fitted a scaffolding system, obtained from a specialist shop. The structure is 2.75 m wide; 1.4 m deep and 2.5 m high (8.8×4.5×8.2 ft) and within its framework is contained a double bed, wardrobe, desk and shelving—even a chair. The platform at the top of the ladder also conveniently acts as access to the loft (out of shot, left). The wardrobe has Venetian blind doors which match the blind at the window, while bright primary colours teamed with grey give the structure a lively, jolly appearance. Built along the wall opposite the scaffolding is a row of cupboards with a fitted washbasin, and these complete a comfortable all-purpose spare room within a severely restricted space.

For anyone on a tight budget, scaffolding is an invaluable system: it can be added to as, and when, you have the money, it is completely flexible to meet your needs and there is the extra bonus that if you get bored with the structure it can be re-adapted and re-used. In fact this is already the case with the scaffolding shown here. Since the photograph was taken, the shelving and desk have been dismantled and re-assembled into a cot to meet the requirements of a new arrival to the family.

SCULPTURED METAL II

BEFORE TWO
LARGE OLD ROOMS

AFTER COMBINED
BEDROOM AND
STUDY/SITTING ROOM

The walls and ceiling of this turn-of-the-century home remain untouched, but sandwiched between them and the floor is a totally new environment.

Having knocked out one bedroom wall to open up the room into a general sitting and study area, the visual break between the two was created by low platforms, a system which also delineates specific areas elsewhere in the apartment. Covered with relatively inexpensive sheet aluminium over a plywood frame, the platforms are practical as well as aesthetic as they house all the necessary services—including electrics—so leaving the walls undisturbed.

The architect has also placed moveable desk lights in an original way so that they seem to grow out of the floor to cast light against the white walls.

The bed is specially designed in polished aluminium, the hole at the foot-rest end being available for plants or for a housing bracket for the television. How is it possible to keep such a bedroom so pure in concept? The answer lies in a dressing room filled with all the usual clutter, located in a sensible spot next to the bathroom and well out of sight, as is another large general storage area behind the bulkhead-like door. The utter visual simplicity of the conversion calls for the same unfussy furnishing treatment. Its unusual but basically neutral background acts as a perfect foil for the pieces of classical modern design which the owner has collected. Each piece is thrown into relief, and the space around it ensures that it can be viewed as well as used.

The ceiling to the bedroom and other areas (for the kitchen, see page 34) will eventually sport a canopy of translucent white cloth, weighted in the middle to make in inverted pyramid shape which will complete the new 'filling' within the old core.

A wall between this room (above) and its neighbour was removed before building of the platforms was begun. Their shiny surfaces reflect sky and artificial light (right) which can give the uncanny impression of walking on air. Simple classic modern furniture is shown off beautifully against such a background.

TECHNIQUES

SANDBLASTING GLASS

Sandblasted glass is useful for overlooked lavatory windows or windows without views where you still need maximum light. The sandblasting technique is simply a way of applying a matt finish to glass which keeps it translucent; most High Street glass merchants offer the service. A temporary sand-blasted look can also be achieved by spraying aluminium paint through stencils. The paint can always be wiped off with the appropriate solvent if you want to change the pattern.

1. Work out the design you want, then cover the glass with self-adhesive plastic film. Draw out your pattern on it with a felt-tip pen.
Alternatively, for simple geometrics and patterns of lines, masking tape can be used.

2. Use a scalpel to cut out the areas you want sandblasted. Then take the panel to the glass merchants who will fire their sandblasting machine at it.

3. Remove the remaining plastic film. Some glass merchants may also offer to fit your panel/window for you if you cannot manage it yourself.

FAKING STAINED GLASS

MAKING ARCHITRAVES

Fake stained glass can look almost as convincing as the sailing boat panel of real stained glass seen here. Most kits comprise a black or grey outlining material or a pliable metal strip which resembles traditional leading. Special translucent stained glass colours can be painted on but look most effective limited to small areas. Large areas of colour are better applied by cutting out shapes in coloured self-adhesive plastic film.

1. Get your chosen design enlarged at a photocopy shop to the correct size for the panel. Trace off the design and place under the glass.

 Architraves can be made up from DIY ready-made wood mouldings and door panels to suit requirements. Complex, elegant detailing of a bygone era can be simulated quite successfully by joining two or three mouldings together with adhesives and plaster. Planing by hand removes or smooths ridges. Alternatively, some specialist DIY shops can now reshape softwood lengths to a particular design so that an exact match can be made to an existing pattern. Corner pieces and door panels can have extra carvings fixed on, made in plastic which look just like wood when painted.

2. Draw out the pattern using the appropriate outlining material.

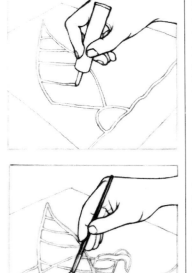

3. Apply colours using a 'flowing' movement similar to painting with nail polish (ie, brush in one direction only, one coat at a time).

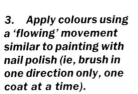

For an architrave like this one you need to make a template of the original moulding. It is easy with an adjustable metal gadget. Better still is a piece of the original moulding. A small section of approximately 35 mm will be enough for a skilled wood machine operator to copy.

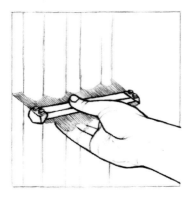

143

RECYCLING A WARDROBE

This handsome, free-standing corner unit in a family bathroom was made from an Edwardian mahogany wardrobe and rebuilt using the services of a professional carpenter. The drawer front now flaps down to store soaps and cleaning utensils, while the three shelves inside are used for towels, etc. Inexperienced woodworkers might wish to follow the example of using a professional joiner. But for those wanting to copy the idea themselves, see steps 1 and 2 opposite.

To make the new cupboard, which was to be painted, a mixture of old and new wood was used. The shaded areas on the drawing (right) show which parts of the old wardrobe were recycled. The new cupboard doors came from the wardrobe's two side panels, but new wood provided the frame.

Before painting, the wood was thoroughly sanded and given a thin coat of primer. Small pots of matt paint were used and blended with a brush to achieve the soft pastel mix effect. As the cupboard was to be sited next to a basin, a matt lacquer was applied to keep the surface free from dirt and splash marks.

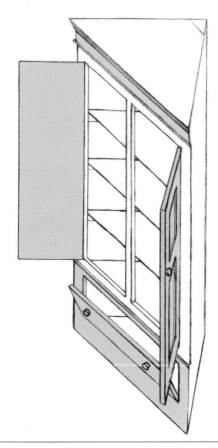

FIREPLACE DOLLS' HOUSE

This dolls' house provides an imaginative, practical answer to an ugly blocked-in chimney in a child's bedroom. Its doors open out to reveal six furnished rooms big enough to take additional toys and general clutter. The whole unit measures approximately 1 m (3 ft) high by 60 cm (2 ft) wide by 30 cm (1 ft) deep. Ingenious details include windows made from picture frames and special dolls' house lighting.

1. Make a box from medium density fibreboard to fit the fireplace opening. Then cut the two shelves, door panels and pediment.

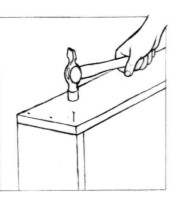

2. Rout out 20 mm (¾ in) slots in the box sides to take the shelves. Use a jigsaw to cut out the window and front door apertures.

3. Cut softwood beading and dowel rod to size for the edge, detailing and porch surround. Fit in picture frames and make up the porch; cut and fix the front door with small cabinet hinges.

1.   **Most corner walls do not make a true 90° angle, so always allow for discrepancies. A solid triangular piece of wood (called an arris) can be used to provide a strong corner plate on which to fix 25 mm by 75 mm (1 in by 3 in) softwood framing. This may need to be planed to fit the exact angle of the corner.**

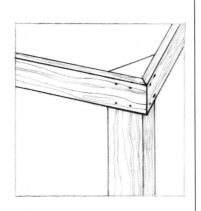

2.   **In-fill panels of 3 mm (⅛ in) thick plywood are lighter and more economical than blockboard or chipboard; inside shelves fixed on battens can be made of these materials and treated with mahogany wood stain if necessary. Use an angle block to cut moulding accurately.**

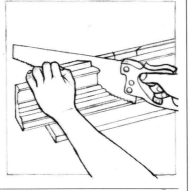

4.   **Sand all over thoroughly before spraying with two coats of white enamel paint. When dry, slot in the shelves; screw on the door panels with piano hinges.**

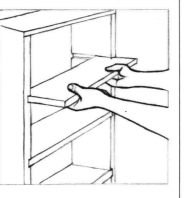

5.   **Fit the box into the fireplace opening. Stick the pediment above with plastic padding and then stick beading detail all the way round.**

AGING A FLOOR

Achieving that coveted 'Old Colonial' patina generally means having to tone down brash new yellow wood. For a very light to white finish you must use a wood bleach—not a wood lightener. Bleaching also makes the wood very alkaline so it must be rinsed off with a solution of 1 part vinegar to every 7 parts water. You can then treat the wood with a wire brush to bring up the grain. A light scim coat of plaster filler should be applied, then sanded off before applying three coats of matt, clear polyurethane varnish,– use thinned down undercoat or gloss paint, as seen on the floorboards below.

1.   **Sand wood thoroughly with medium grade steel wool or sandpaper. Apply a coat of thinned down gloss paint—white, pale grey or blue are all convincing as 'aged' colours. Mix 1 part white spirit to 2 parts paint.**

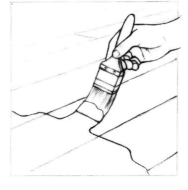

2.   **When dry apply a second coat of thinned paint, adding a little more white spirit to make the colour a shade lighter. Brush this roughly down the middle of each floorboard for an authentic well trodden look. Finish with two coats of clear matt polyurethane varnish.**

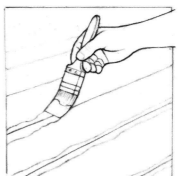

145

PAINTED RUG FRAME

A painted rug frame is an ingenious way to make the most of a modest carpet or rug bargain and establish the floor as a focal point. When painting floor patterns you need to use fast-drying as well as hard-wearing paint. Tubes of PVA paint come in a good range of colours and dilute readily with water for a transparent finish. Used neat, they are opaque, but two or three coats may be needed on some colours. Always seal surfaces afterwards with at least three coats of either polyurethane varnish or colourless varnish.

1. If floorboards are old, check each one carefully, nailing those that are loose (using floor or oval nails) approximately 3 mm (⅛ in) from the edge of the board along the line of the joists. If hiring a sander you will also need to go over the whole floor—knock all nails down to save wear and tear.

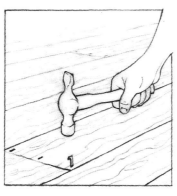

2. Sand thoroughly starting with medium grade sandpaper or steel wool, working through to the finest grade. Always sand with the grain to prevent marking. Before applying any new paint (or varnish) the wood must be free of all old polishes and coatings or paint will not adhere.

3. Apply two coats of gloss paint. The paint used here was not thinned but this is a matter of preference. Allow overnight drying between coats, or even longer in some cases, depending on the paint and drying conditions.

4. Decide where you will be putting your rug, then when the paint is dry, draw a rectangle (or a square) to rug size. Mark the area with masking tape to help keep your painted edges straight. Place another line of masking tape approximately 30 cm (12 in) away to form the outer edge of the frame.

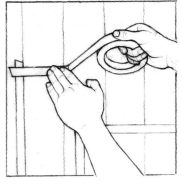

5. Fauvist-style stripes were painted here with PVA colours. If you want straight stripes use masking tape to keep the edges neat. New colours can be mixed on old white saucers or old margarine tubs. Give the floor three coats of colourless sealer or plastic coating to finish.

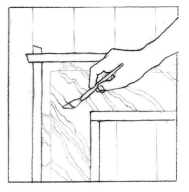

PALAZZO FLOOR

The painted tile design on this floor was inspired by a much grander version seen in an Italian palace. Here, the old wooden boards were sanded thoroughly but some dents and chips were left to retain an authentic-looking antique patina. Before painting, prepare the surface, check for loose boards and sand thoroughly either with a sander or by hand. Seal the floor all over with a coat of clear, matt polyurethane varnish thinned down with white spirit. When dry, sand again with the finest grade sandpaper.

4. *Draw in the diagonals of each square. Use masking tape to demark the lines and keep any varnished and painted edges straight. Paint in the white squares first, using two coats of white undercoat thinned down with white spirit.*

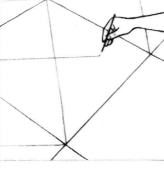
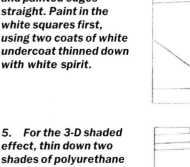

1. *Work out the tile design by centring and squaring up, then use squared paper to do a scale drawing of your floor plan. You may need to alter the size of your tile design to fit complete tiles into the area. Or leave space at the edges for a border of complementary pattern.*

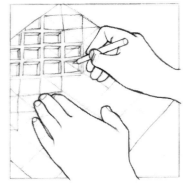

5. *For the 3-D shaded effect, thin down two shades of polyurethane varnish with white spirit. Use a varnish brush to paint the light shade in first, then the dark. Sand when dry and apply the second coat. After drying out, apply three coats of clear, matt polyurethane varnish.*

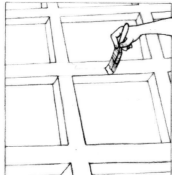

2. *To find the floor centre, mark the centres of two opposite walls; place a heavily chalked string across the floor, and then draw a line. Repeat for the opposite walls. The point at which both lines intersect is the centre.*

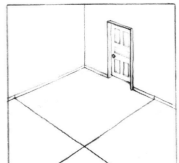

3. *Working from the floor centre, measure one tile square and mark off points along the lines of intersection. Draw lines between the points. Check that the squares are accurate by measuring the corners with a right angle. A T-square is useful for large areas.*

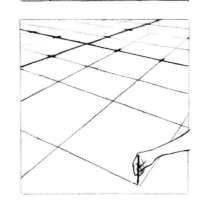

STENCILLING FLOORS

Stencils can do a great deal for such humble floor coverings as plain hardboard or chipboard. The technique for stencilling floors is similar to that used for walls, although the scale is usually larger and patterns have to be particularly easy on the eye at floor level. Border stencils for floors offer great scope for those wishing to point up a particularly beautiful rug, and are a good deal less taxing than stencilling a whole floor.

Floors to be stencilled, whatever the material, must have smooth surfaces. Paint them with two thinned coats of undercoat or gloss, or seal them with polyurethane varnish. Take care that the stencil's dye, stain, or paint does not react with the preparation coat. Make a test trial with your materials on a separate piece of wood before you start stencilling.

Avoid using stencil brushes over large areas; it is tiring on the back and arms. Extra pressure caused by bending tends to result in heavier brushwork and blurred stencil edges, although this can add rustic charm to the result.

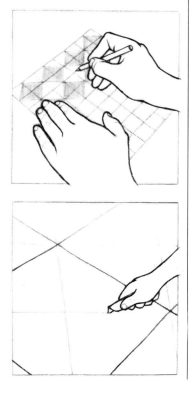

1. Designs for floors tend to be larger and more geometric than those for walls. Simple tile design stencils are probably the easiest to start with. For centring and squaring up patterns, see page 147. Floor stencils also need to be worked in fast-drying colours.

2. Scoring patterns with a sharp knife helps to prevent colours from bleeding. Waterproof felt pens, inks and wood stains let the wood grain show through. Spray-on gloss paint cans must be held at an angle or else the nozzle will clog. Acrylic and PVA paints need at least three coats of varnish.

METAL HAMMERED FINISH

This type of finish can be instantly achieved with special, siliconized hammered metal paint. Originally developed as an anti-rust agent, the paint can miraculously transform metal, wood (painted or unprimed) as well as plastic. As the paint dries in around 15–20 minutes after application it is excellent for revamping elderly kitchen appliances such as refrigerators and spin-driers.

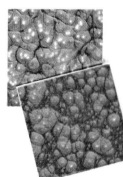

1. To apply hammered metal paint, all surfaces should be grease and dirt free. Any flaking rust should be removed by sanding.

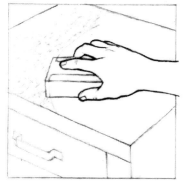

2. Stir contents of the tin well, as pigment tends to settle. Use a disposable paint brush when applying as special solvent is needed although petrol works quite well. Brush on the paint fairly thickly but do not allow any drips to form. On non-horizontal surfaces, apply slightly less paint in a stabbing movement.

3. Wait 20 minutes or so and apply a second coat. The second coat should be applied the same day; if this is not possible wait at least a month. Try and cover smallish areas at a time, approximately 60 cm square; work in panels on larger areas and use a paint roller with disposable foam pads.

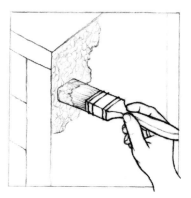

PAINTING FURNITURE

Painting a junk shop table and random odd chairs in the same colours and patterns gives the impression of a matching set. The table and chair here were painted freehand using PVA paints. Instead of protecting the finish with polyurethane varnish, all of which contain some yellow colouring that affects final paint colours (eg, blues turne green and whites yellow), colourless clear, cold cure acid-hardened lacquer (Plastic Coating) was used. This gives heavy-duty protection so is also eminently suited to kitchen table tops. For painted furniture needing less protection, art shops sell a variety of colour-free acrylic varnishes used for protecting oil paintings.

1. Rub down surfaces using steel wool or sandpaper, working through from medium to finest grades. Steel wool is particularly effective on mouldings and carvings. Fill any gaps and cracks with plastic wood, then paint furniture all over with wood primer to seal any bare wood and filler.

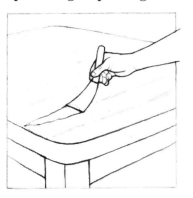

2. Sand all over when dry with fine grade sandpaper. Apply two coats of undercoat thinned down with white spirit—you can also use emulsion paint thinned with a little water. Sand lightly between coats with finest grade sandpaper.

3. Draw out your design with a pencil. Fix low-tack masking tape over any areas or patterns that need straight edges (ie, geometric shapes).

4. Mix up PVA paint colours on clean white saucers and use artists' bristle brushes to paint on patterns. When paints are dry (around 20 minutes), go over areas where painted colours are thin—some may need at least five coats before enough density is achieved. Leave painted surfaces to dry.

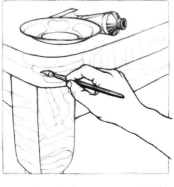

5. Using a varnish brush, apply the first coat of colour-free Plastic Coating or acrylic varnish. Press overloaded bristles against the side of the can; don't drag across the rim as this causes bubbles. Sand between coats, lightly removing any dust with a tack rag. Three coats should be adequate.

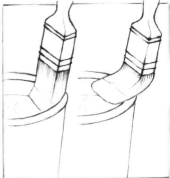

MARBLING FURNITURE

Who would ever guess that this elegant dining table was once a humble junk shop bargain? Thanks to the professional handiwork of two expert marblers even its bulbous legs look beautiful. But first study the marble you want to copy as there are eight categories; keep a small piece for reference while you work to make your efforts look realistic. It also helps to have another pair of hands available whilst applying the glaze—it needs to be worked in quickly while wet. Always start from the lightest colour glazes and work through to the dark. For simulating the transparency of a real marble, cream, beige, rust and dark brown glazes were used.

1. Prepare wood by sanding down thoroughly; bare wood should be primed with wood primer and then sanded with finest grade paper.

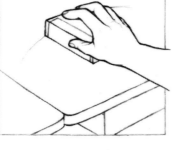

2. Apply two coats of cream gloss undercoat thinned down with white spirit.

3. Apply the first glaze in 4 to 5 dabs working diagonally across the top panels to imitate the veins of real marble.

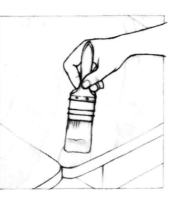

4. Take a small chamois or small natural sea sponge (make-up sponges are ideal) and wring it out in white spirit; dab lightly at the glazing to soften and fade any hard edges.

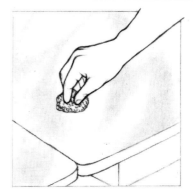

6. *Use a No 2 artist's brush and some white paint to fidget in the final veins. Finally, while the paint is still wet, go over the entire surface very lightly with a dry brush to blend in any remaining hard edges.*

SPONGING

7. *The table top's edges and stretchers were then sponged with a coat of pale glaze: 1 part cream undercoat to 2 parts white spirit.*

8. *Again, soak the sponge in white spirit, wring it out well, dip it into the glaze and wring it out again before applying.*
Sponge the edges, then the stretchers in a regular, scalloped pattern. Cover all the gaps but leave some background showing through.

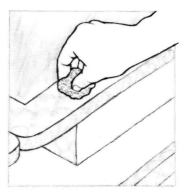

5. *Take a No 12 artist's brush, or a dusting brush and build up the glazing lines gradually. Then go across and put some colour on the light ground. Continue this sponging and brushing technique. Finally use a dry artist's brush (No 2 to 4) to 'fidget' in the veins. Apply the final glaze colour sparingly, working well in with a sponge.*

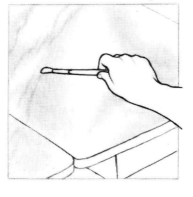

9. *Two or three shades of extra colour add zest to the pattern, but wait until each colour is dry before applying the next. The whole table should then be given three coats of glossy polyurethane varnish for protection.*

INSTANT MARBLING

Less-than-elegant cast iron, plaster or concrete mantelpieces and surrounds can be successfully disguised by clever painting. As with the marbled table (previous page) it is useful to have a piece or photograph of the marble you wish to copy for a working reference. The difference in this technique is that emulsion and fast-drying acrylic paints are used. The results may be less realistic but are quicker.

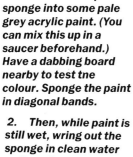

3.   With an artist's brush (No 2 to 4) lightly 'fidget' (paint shakily) in the veins in a slightly darker grey.

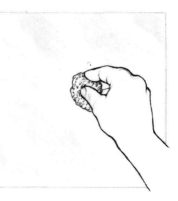

4.   When dry, smudge these over with a little white acrylic paint on a damp sponge. 'Fidget' in some faint veins—these can be a greyish beige if you wish.

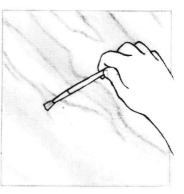

1.   Apply two coats of white emulsion to a clean surface. When dry, sand with fine grade sandpaper. Dip the edge of a small make-up sponge into some pale grey acrylic paint. (You can mix this up in a saucer beforehand.) Have a dabbing board nearby to test tne colour. Sponge the paint in diagonal bands.

2.   Then, while paint is still wet, wring out the sponge in clean water and gently smudge and blot over the bands so that there are no harsh edges. Sand surfaces with finest grade sandpaper between applications.

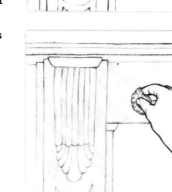

5.   Repeat the dry sponging technique using diluted white acrylic paint and covering all areas so that some are seen to be more faded than others. Allow to dry out thoroughly.

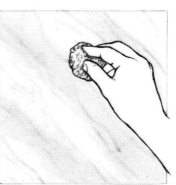

6.   Sand lightly with finest grade sandpaper before giving two coats of matt acrylic varnish. For an authentic marble sheen, buff and dry varnished surface with powdered French chalk or flour.

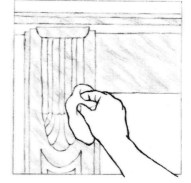

PAINTED FREIZES

This is an economic and pretty way to lower a high ceiling visually. Here, a hand-painted neo-classical swag border in a child's bedroom cleverly links the striped walls, bedcover and Napoleonic bed. The design was inspired by a similar one in the home of the early 20th-century Swedish illustrator, Carl Larsson.

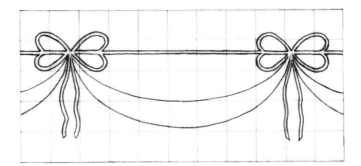

1. Measure length of wall and work out where swag semicircles will come. Use an oval serving dish as a template. Be particularly careful at corners—the swags do not have to end abruptly. Here, the designer has carried the swag round, placing it slightly off centre.

2. Mix powder paints and add a little gum arabic to bind the colour if necessary. Poster paints, acrylic or gouache paints will also do. For painting thin lines, a lining brush can be useful, but practise first on paper. A fine sable brush and a steady hand are all you really need.

SPECIAL EFFECTS

Gold walls are a lot easier and cheaper to decorate than in the 1920s, when real gold and silver leaf were applied. Today we can use gold foil papers, or sprinkle gold glitter powders on to lining paper coated with wallpaper adhesives. Decoupage papers are easy to do; the gold one here adds considerable cachet to plain, pale green emulsion-painted walls. A complementary frieze gives a tailored finish.

STAIRWAY MURALS

Hallways need not be gloomy places you want to walk through as quickly as possible. Decorative techniques, including hand-painted patterns, friezes, or, as here, stylized ducks, add a distinctive touch to what might otherwise be drab and colourless entrances.

1. Buy a few sheets of self-adhesive gold foil paper—available from specialized paper shops. Cut out shapes, either random or regular according to the look you want.

1. Choose a suitable design. Simple, bold motifs are easiest and quickest. The ducks here were inspired by some Egyptian/Iranian folk paintings seen in a book. Decide the size you want and take your visual references along to a photocopier to enlarge.

2. Peel off protective backing from each piece as it is needed and smooth down well on the wall with your hands. Work over small areas at a time.

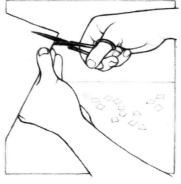

2. The enlarged copies can then be traced directly on to a wall or a piece of stencil board. If you are planning only a few motifs, you can cover the enlarged pattern with self-adhesive clear film and cut out the pattern with a sharp scalpel as you would for a stencil.

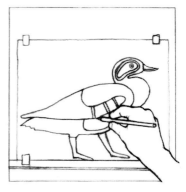

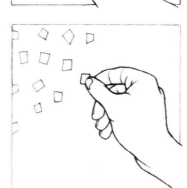

3. Spray the back of your stencil board of plastic covered print with mount adhesive to prevent paint seeping underneath. Paints can be PVA, acrylic or poster but in this case, small pots of pastel-coloured emulsions were used. Shading was done with dark green emulsion.

FABRIC-COVERED FURNITURE

This is artful camouflage for badly worn surfaces, but for best results the table should be a simple cube or console shape. There are two basic methods for covering. For the first you will need a special display artist's staple gun (the ordinary office stationery type uses the wrong sort of staples); a staple remover is useful too, as it takes out staples without damaging the surrounding fabric.

The second method is suitable for tables with more complex mouldings and shapes, but for these the fabric should be thinner—cotton, lawn or pure silk, for example. Instead of stapling, wallpaper adhesive is used. Rough table surfaces give better adhesion than smooth ones, so plastic and laminate materials should first be scored or sanded with coarse paper. Fabrics may darken slightly with the adhesive, but raw edges are also prevented from fraying.

1. **Make a paper template of the whole table. Ideally, the fabric should be cut out in one piece (several pieces mean more visible joins) so expect a fair amount of wastage. Allow about 25 mm (1 in) all round for fabric overlap.**

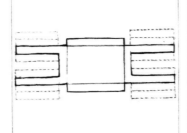

2. **Cut out the fabric and place over the table top, smoothing it as taut as possible. Staple the overhang underneath. Then, working from opposite corners, pleat or fold the excess fabric and staple in place.**

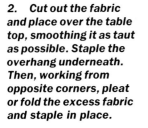

3. **Wrap fabric round each leg, stapling down the inside back. If joins cannot be avoided, hide them beneath braid stuck on with clear fabric adhesive.**

1. **Make a template as before and cut out fabric. Mix up some regular wallpaper adhesive (not heavy duty) using 1 heaped teaspoon to half a pint of water. Leave for 30 minutes before using.**

2. **Brush the adhesive liberally on to table surfaces and place fabric on top (it should become saturated). Smooth fabric with a brush and more paste, folding and pleating excess. Cut darts to make a snug fit around mouldings or awkward shapes. Allow 24 hours to dry.**

3. **To protect fabric table tops, treat with a spray-on stain repellent; specially-cut glass tops will also give protection.**

FABRIC AS WALLS

The ruched fabric screens in the photograph on pages 130–131 are an ingenious way to divide up bedsitter open-plan living activities into eating, sleeping and washing areas. They provide a distinct improvement on non-flexible hardboard partitions that can make small rooms feel claustrophobic.

1. Choose a fabric that pleats easily. Most cottons and silks are fine and will wash easily. Furnishing cottons are wider and tend to be in thicker weights than dress cottons—and are also less see-through. Allow twice the fabric width for each pole (ie, 20 ft fabric: 10 ft pole). Hem fabric lengths at top and base.

2. Hem fabric lengths at top and base. Then thread through a 12 mm (½ in) diameter dowel rod.

3. Fix metal dowel supports to floors and ceilings at approximately 1 metre intervals.

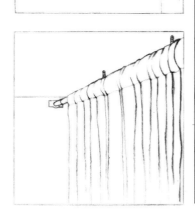

CLEANING A CORNICE

This decorative detail of a plaster flower is from a ceiling border obscured by twenty coats of distemper about 6 mm thick. For cleaning, use the following method:-

1. Lever off gently with a paint scraper or a hammer and chisel—removing items first makes them much easier to clean than if they are left in situ; working at a height is tiring on the arms.

2. Leave to soak overnight in a bucket of water; clean off any stubborn paint traces with an orange stick and nail file.

3. Leave to dry out thoroughly before painting with shellac and fixing with a two-part epoxy resin cement or plastic padding.

CLEANING A CEILING ROSE

The owner of this plasterwork (dating from about 1820) had a pleasant surprise on discovering that the fitting unscrewed quite easily for cleaning. Not all do, and those that are plastered in are best left. It is also a good idea to check that any original fixings are safe. Replace them if necessary. When repainting, consider two tones of the same colour: pale almond green and ecru; or magnolia and shell pink, rather than predictable white.

1. *Soak fitting overnight—if possible in the bath. Then gently scrub at old paintwork with a toothbrush; a nail file is useful for unclogging the fiddly bits.*

2. *Seal bare plaster with a coat of shellac varnish before repainting. This will prevent paint sinking in. Repaint before fixing back on ceiling.*

INDEX

ACKNOWLEDGEMENTS

Owners/designers

8-9 Brian Taggart of Brian Taggart Associates; 10-11 Charles Rutherford; 12-13 Maureen Walker; 14-15 Douglas Hamilton for Mr & Mrs Peters; 16-17 Piers Gough of Campbell Zagolovitch Wilkinson & Gough for Carol McNicoll; 18-19 Geoffrey Harris of London Lighting; 20-21 Pat and Mike Fawcett; 22-23 Judy and Neil Bardrick; 24-25 Joan Fitzler for Suzanne Lowry; 26-27 top right, Maureen Walker; bottom, Roger Hammond; main pic, (rug) John Canning; top right, Sanderson & Son; bottom right, Angela Hunt of Angela Hunt Textiles; 28-29 Siris/Coombs Architects, New York; 30-31 Henrietta Green; 32-33 John Rushton; 34-35 Jan Kaplicky and David Nixon of Future Systems for Deyan Sudjic; 36-37 Hunt Thompson Associates; 38-39 Brigitta Muller; 40-41 Brigitta Muller; 42-43 John Edwards of Pollard Thomas Edwards & Associates; 44-45 Angus Bruce of Angus John Bruce & Co., New York; 46-47 Oliver Morgan of Morgan & Grzegorczyk; 48 left, Charles Rutherford; main pic, Brigitta Muller; 49 top, Bronson Shaw; right, Jon Weallans; 50-51 Geoffrey Harris of London Lighting; 52-53 Tony Babarik; 54-55 Pauline and John Larkin; 56-57 Pauline and John Larkin; 58-59 Maureen Walker; 60-61 Eva Jiricna; 62-63 Caroline Quartermaine; 64-65 Brigitta Muller; 66-67 Brigitta Muller; 68-69 Chrissie and Chris Hesford of Astrohome; 70-71 Options; 74-75 bottom right, Andrew Holmes; top right, Johnny Grey Design; middle, Judith and Graham Robinson; main pic, Brigitta Muller; 76-77

McDonough Rainey, New York; 78-79 Piers Gough of Campbell Zagolovitch Wilkinson & Gough; 80-81 Clive Evans Design Consultants; 82-83 Graham Carr; 84-85 Simon Conder for Wendy Booth & Leslie Howell; 86-87 Mark Foley of Burrell Foley Associates; 88 top left, Angela Hunt; top right, Roger Hammond; 89 top, Tony Babarik; bottom, Pauline & John Larkin; 92-93 left, Mark Foley of Burrell Foley Associates; right, Martin Wagner; 94 Jonathan Gale of Gale & Prior Architects; 95 main pic, Angus Bruce, Julyan Wickham; 96-97 Brigitta Muller; 98-99 main pic, Lynne and Richard Bryant; top right, Roger Hammond; 100 top right, Pauline and John Larkin; 101 Maureen Walker; 102-103 Camera Press; 104-105 Clive Evans Design Consultants; 106-107 Sally & Charles Settrington; 108-109 Clive Evans Design Consultants; 110-111 Sunday Times; 112-113 Henrietta Green; 114-115 Brigitta Muller; 116-117 Brian Taggart of Brian Taggart Associates; 118-119 Carol McNicoll; 120-121 Angus Bruce of Angus John Bruce & Co, New York; 122-123 Eva Jiricna; 124-125 Siris/Coombs Architects, New York; 126 Roger Hammond; 127 top, David Bentheim; bottom, Simon Conder; 128-129 Chrissie & Chris Hesford; 130-131 Tony Babarik; 132-133 Tony Babarik; 134-135 Malcolm Pawley for Hilary Symonds and Dave Watters of Flying Saucer; 136-137 left, Fred Scott; right, Eva Jiricna; 138-139 Tim Leyland; 140-141 Jan Kaplicky and David Nixon of Future Systems for Deyan Sudjic; 142-143 left, Sanderson & Sons; 146-147 left, Angela

Hunt; right, Graham Carr; 150-151 paint by Dulux; 152-153 marbling by Georgina Chetwode and Vicky Ellerton

Photographic credits

8-9 Brian Taggart; 10 Simon Battensby; 11 Dave King; 12 Simon Battensby; 13 Victor Watts; 14 Victor Watts; 15 Victor Watts; 16-17 Victor Watts; 18-19 Victor Watts; 20-21 Dave King; 22-23 Victor Watts; 24-25 Clive Frost; 26 Victor Watts (Top right) Grub Street (Bottom); 27 – Karen Bussolini Main pic – Sanderson (Top right) Angela Hunt (Bottom right); 28-29 Joe Standart; 30-31 Jessica Strang; 32-33 Dave King; 34-35 Dave King; 36-37 Martin Charles/Hunt Thompson Assoc; 38-39 Victor Watts; 40-41 Victor Watts; 42 John Edwards; 43 Victor Watts; 44-45 Dorothea Schwarzhaupt; 46-47 Jessica Strang; 48 Dave King (Left) Jessica Strang (Top right); 49 Victor Watts; 50-51 Victor Watts; 52-53 Victor Watts; 54-55 Victor Watts; 55-56 Victor Watts; 56-57 Victor Watts; 58-59 Frank Thurston; 60-61 Richard Bryant; 62-63 Victor Watts; 64-65 Victor Watts; 66-67 Victor Watts; 68-69 Victor Watts; 70-71 Syndication International; 72-73 Morley-Steinberg; 74 Simon Battensby (Middle pic); 75 Victor Watts; 76-77 Nick Wheeler; 78-79 Christine Hanscomb; 80-81 Clive Evans; 82-83 Dave King; 84-85 Clive Evans; 86-87 Mark Foley; 88 Angela Hunt (Left); Bottom Simon Battensby (Right); 89 Victor Watts; 92 Mark Foley; 93 Martin Wagner; 102-103 Camera Press; 104-105 Steve Bicknell; 106-107 Dave King; 108-109 Steve Bicknell; 110-111 James Mortimer; 112-113 Jessica Strang; 114-115 Victor Watts; Jessica Strang (Bottom Right); 116-117 Brian Taggart;

118-119 Victor Watts; 120-121 Angus Bruce; 122-123 Richard Bryant; 124-125 Roger Bester; 126 (Left); Frank Thurston; Jessica Strang; Clive Crook (Bottom); 128-129 Victor Watts; 130-131 Victor Watts; 132-133 Victor Watts; 134-135 Victor Watts; 136 Di Lewis; 137 Richard Bryant; 138-139 Clive Frost; 140-141 Dave King; 142-143 Roger Daniells, Simon Battensby; 144-145 Roger Hammond; 146 Angela Hunt; 147 Dave King; 149 Angela Hunt; 150-151 Frank Thurston; 152-153 Frank Thurston; 154 Christine Hanscomb; 155 Lucinda Lambton; 157 Roger Hammond; 158 Roger Hammond.

All pictures taken by:
Victor Watts
Simon Battensby
Dave King
Frank Thurston
Copyright Grub Street.

Plan drawings by Hussein Hussein. Technique drawings by Lynette Conway.

Our thanks go to The Conran Shop for some of the items featured on the front jacket photograph.